Praise for
Taught Me to Fly

"I believe we can find God in many ways," writes Ashley Mae Hoiland, and her remarkable volume bears out that belief in both content and form. In fjords and in forests, in mission and in motherhood, Hoiland susses out traces of the divine. Her purpose is not to define God, but rather to find God in all God's resistance to definition. Hoiland's imagistic, candid reflections, unfolding without the constraint of linear narrative, perform their devotions from oblique angles and shifting stances. The insights that accumulate on the wings of these *One Hundred Birds* are—we come to realize as we read into and around in them—not distinguishable from the process of attention that allows such insight to flourish, to transform both the thing attended to and the one who attends. There's a word for that kind of attention—it's *reverence*.

—Kimberly Johnson
Author of *Uncommon Prayer: Poems*

Ashley Mae Hoiland cracks open her heart in this book and reveals a singular Mormon experience that, in all its joy, pain, and complication, we recognize as our own. She gives us illustrations, poetry, and prose in vivid vignettes—pictures in words that, in their kaleidoscopic total, capture the lived reality of Mormon life far more richly than any one of those things could in isolation. By taking us through her childhood conversion, her youth, her mission, single adulthood, and the exquisite emotions of motherhood, she shows that religious life is about *living* far more than it is about *believing*. The lifeblood of her faith pulses through these pages.

—MATTHEW BOWMAN
Author of *The Mormon People: The Making of an American Faith*

This brave collection of revelatory meditations and illustrations traverses Ashley Mae Hoiland's unique spiritual landscape. Feeling that she has lost God hundreds of times, she finds him again in personal episodes, relationships, nature, dreams, imagination, stories, scriptures, memory, and testimony. These turn her from a life in crisis to one of ongoing exploration. The reader can find herself in this search and these pictures.

—CLAUDIA L. BUSHMAN
Author of *Contemporary Mormonism: Latter-day Saints in Modern America*

Ashley Mae Hoiland has found God in places that most of us never think to look: in cruelty and poverty, in emptiness and desire, and in people whose divinity is buried deep within all-too-human frames. She shapes her stories of searching and discovery into elegant prose poems recalling the work of Sandra Cisneros and Terry Tempest Williams. But Hoiland's voice is wholly original. Her journeys through landscapes of faith end in neither certainty nor doubt, but in a mature and reflective faith at home in the spaces between. Contemporary Mormonism needs Hoiland's stories and example. In this compulsively readable work of art, she teaches us how to turn the raw experiences of a life into beautiful things, and then she shows us, as only a true artist can, how those beautiful things can also be holy.

—MICHAEL AUSTIN
Author of *Re-reading Job: Understanding the Ancient World's Greatest Poem*

This book powerfully illustrates the truth that the rich tapestry of our lives and faith is woven of thousands of small moments—the joyful, the painful, and the mundane. Hoiland's stories inspire us not only to recognize the grace and power of these small moments, but also to examine and find within them our own voice and capacity for greatness. Her journey is a beautiful reminder that by embracing the tension between faith and doubt we can move beneath the superficial surface to a place of godliness. Her words inspire me to extend more grace—to others and to myself.

—DIANNE R. ORCUTT
Cofounder of Aspiring Mormon Women

Discussions about challenges in contemporary Mormonism often fall into predictable patterns, both in content and in structure. Ashley Mae Hoiland's gorgeously written reflections situate themselves quite to the side of the usual debates. Instead of giving answers, Hoiland describes a deeply personal process of spirituality. By inviting readers to accompany her along the spiritual side paths of everyday life, she shows them how connection to God and to other people can emerge from creative attention to the ordinary. Spiritual life, she suggests, is a quiet sort of art. Opportunities to create it abound, especially in the quotidian relationships that are the basic stuff of our lives. This book provides an occasion to study that art with one of its understated masters. I commend it—and her—to you.

—JASON A. KERR
Assistant Professor of English,
Brigham Young University

As Terry Tempest Williams observed, "Mormon women write. This is what we do, we write for posterity, noting the daily happenings of our lives. Keeping a journal is keeping a record." *One Hundred Birds Taught Me to Fly* is the record of a Mormon woman striving in big and small ways to find God in daily happenings, big and small. Ashley Mae Hoiland's tiny heartfelt stories and remembrances weave in and out to form a larger spiritual narrative with honesty, bravery, and vulnerability. Immeasurably beautiful.

—RACHEL HUNT STEENBLIK
Coeditor of *Mormon Feminism:
Essential Writings*

Ashley Mae Hoiland writes with authenticity and grace. Her pages contain a profoundly affecting memoir. In telling it she plies a nonlinear format with all the sensibilities of an artist and a storyteller's eye for detail. Intimate and vulnerable, she is Mormonism's Anne Morrow Lindbergh.

—RUSSELL HANCOCK
Lecturer in Public Policy, Stanford University

Here is a book where the word is made flesh. This account of Mormon spirituality isn't abstracted from living; it brings us directly into the very interstices of daily encounters with beauty, laughter, sorrow, and grace, where divinity resides. It is more than a plea to live with questions. It is a testament to the fact that, as Hoiland puts it, the "quietness of God is trust," and that in our stories—flawed and raw and seemingly chaotic—can be found the sacraments of renewal if we but learn to see our lives with greater compassion and deeper gratitude. Hoiland offers us a healing book for troubled times.

—GEORGE B. HANDLEY
Author of *Home Waters: A Year of Recompenses on the Provo River*

We live in days when debates over history, politics, and cultural issues absorb the attention of many Mormon thinkers, sometimes at the expense of careful attention to the quiet rhythms of Mormon living. But what if peace in our lives and communities is not to be found by identifying the "right" positions so much as by reawakening the often-neglected Mormon imagination? In *One Hundred Birds Taught Me to Fly*, Ashley Mae Hoiland turns her artistic vision and lyrical power toward her Mormon life, weaving together memories—of both significant occasions and fleeting everyday perceptions—in an attempt to capture "the sacred writ of [her] life." It's work that doubly blesses the reader: by giving us a glimpse into another's spiritual life and by encouraging us to pay more imaginative attention to our own.

—JAMES GOLDBERG
Author of *The Five Books of Jesus*

In an age of rare originality, Ashley Mae Hoiland manages to explore one of the last frontiers of Mormonism: the search for the divine feminine. Her encounters with feminine spiritual forces are so entwined with the language, experiences, and resources of Mormonism that we recognize them as having been there all along, while at the same time being revelations of something entirely new. Hoiland's spiritual autobiography is a revolution in Mormon testimony, describing faith journeying in uniquely fresh and authentic imagery. Absolutely beautiful.

—NEYLAN MCBAINE
Author of *Women at Church: Magnifying LDS Women's Local Impact*

The Mormon belief that God speaks to us according to our own language and unto our understanding is beautifully represented in this unique composition. To Ashley Mae Hoiland, God speaks in prose, poetry, and art to convey truths—both hidden and uncovered. For those of us who know the language of the creative thinker, Hoiland's work becomes a transcription of divinity.

—C. JANE KENDRICK
Author at cjanekendrick.com

This is simply the most artful and perceptive writing about Mormonism I have encountered in a long, long time. The impressionistic glimpses that Ashley Mae Hoiland offers into her experience as a Latter-day Saint woman are clear-eyed, generous, and moving. Through her eyes one gets a sense not only of delight in the beauty of the world and in the love and power of a Heavenly Father and Mother, but also mourning for the loneliness and difficulty that shape human experience, often in such uneven ways. Hoiland's deep love and appreciation for Mormonism, "the house whose halls I know best," shines forth from every page, alongside her loyal sympathy for those who carry deep wounds from their encounters at church. Hoiland's accounts of teenage spiritual searching, missionary adventure, motherhood, and her wrestle with gender issues in Mormon culture are familiar yet startlingly luminous as she paints a tender, sympathetic portrait of the many fellow travelers who have lifted and taught her along the way.

—MELISSA WEI-TSING INOUYE
Associate editor of the *Mormon Studies Review*

Through her exquisite poetry and prose, Ashley Mae Hoiland offers what she aptly terms "the sacred writ of my life." Her intensely personal stories capture the experiences of daughter, sister, wife, mother, missionary, friend, and stranger—all framed within her thoughtful explorations of belief and being. This spiritual autobiography is richly textured with honesty, compassion, and reverence. There is no trite homily here, but rather an abundance of finely turned phrases to ponder. The spare words make their own music while simple line drawings accentuate the poet's artistry. Hoiland's reflections are very female and very Mormon, but she sounds a universal ring in her struggle to find God and embrace all God's children in a world that "both is and is not perfect." There is wonder here, and wholeness and holiness, that carries the reader into his or her own soul.

—JILL MULVAY DERR
Coeditor of *Eliza R. Snow: The Complete Poetry*

With a rare combination of rawness and transcendence, Ashley Mae Hoiland courageously weaves personal stories and visual art into an awe-inspiring tapestry infused with faith. Her ability to mine the depths of everyday moments to discover the grandeur in the messiness of Mormonism and of womanhood makes this book a rare treasure. *One Hundred Birds Taught Me to Fly* moves the deepest parts of my soul unlike any book I have ever read. Ashley Mae's story is my story. It is our story. And I thank her for offering it so generously and for telling it so beautifully.

—JULIE DE AZEVEDO HANKS
Author of *The Assertiveness Guide for Women: How to Communicate Your Needs, Set Healthy Boundaries, and Transform Your Relationships*

Interweaving the personal with the prophetic, *One Hundred Birds Taught Me to Fly* invokes the deepest questions about the foundations of faith. It is a written reflection of the push and pull of emotions and actions that shape who we are within our own personal journeys. Ashley Mae Hoiland's vulnerability in her writing strengthens her invitation to examine how faith bends and stretches over the course of one's life. In doing so, she offers a sweeping narrative of a passage not too far from our own.

—JANAN GRAHAM-RUSSELL
Writer, A Life Diasporatic Blog

One Hundred Birds Taught Me to Fly

A
Living Faith
Book

LIVING FAITH books are for readers who cherish the life of the mind and the things of the Spirit. Each title is a unique example of faith in search of understanding, the voice of a scholar who has cultivated a believing heart while engaged in the disciplines of the Academy.

Other LIVING FAITH books include:

Adam S. Miller, *Letters to a Young Mormon*

Samuel M. Brown, *First Principles and Ordinances: The Fourth Article of Faith in Light of the Temple*

Stephen L. Peck, *Evolving Faith: Wanderings of a Mormon Biologist*

Patrick Q. Mason, *Planted: Belief and Belonging in an Age of Doubt*

Thomas F. Rogers, *Let Your Hearts and Minds Expand: Reflections on Faith, Reason, Charity, and Beauty*

One Hundred Birds Taught Me to Fly

The Art of Seeking God

Ashley Mae Hoiland

NEAL A. MAXWELL
INSTITUTE *for*
RELIGIOUS SCHOLARSHIP

Brigham Young University
Provo, Utah

A LIVING FAITH book
Neal A. Maxwell Institute, Provo 84602 | maxwellinstitute.byu.edu

Printed in the United States of America

Library of Congress Cataloging-in-Publication Data

Names: Hoiland, Ashley Mae, 1984– author, artist.
Title: One hundred birds taught me to fly : the art of seeking God / Ashley Mae
   Hoiland.
Other titles: Living faith book (Neal A. Maxwell Institute for Religious Scholarship)
Description: Provo, Utah : Neal A. Maxwell Institute for Religious Scholarship,
   Brigham Young University, [2016] | Series: A living faith book
Identifiers: LCCN 2016031371 (print) | LCCN 2016032858 (ebook) |
   ISBN 9780842529921 (print : alk. paper) | ISBN 9780842529938 (ePub) |
   ISBN 9780842529945 (Kindle)
Subjects: LCSH: God (Christianity)—Worship and love. | God (Christianity)—
   Knowableness. | Mormon Church—Doctrines. | Church of Jesus Christ of
   Latter-day Saints—Doctrines. | LCGFT: Devotional literature.
Classification: LCC BV4817 .H65 2016 (print) | LCC BV4817 (ebook) |
   DDC 248.4/89332—dc23
LC record available at https://lccn.loc.gov/2016031371

Cover design: Ashley Mae Hoiland and Blair Hodges
Title Calligraphy: Mason Alley Calligraphy

♾ This paper meets the requirements of ANSI/NISO Z39.48-1992
(Permanence of Paper).

CONTENTS

FOREWORD

I came to know Ashley Mae Hoiland (whom I've come to call "Ashmae") through her work before I ever really knew her as a person. I first met her at a local art show when I bought one of her paintings—a mixed-media piece that spoke to me of an individual's search for home. The second time I met Ashmae was at a poetry reading she gave. I was struck by the way her words communicated both vulnerability and strength at the same time. The third time I met Ashmae was at a gathering to celebrate the billboard poetry project she'd helmed—a public initiative that replaced crass billboard advertising with poems, offering drivers a glimpse of beauty in an unexpected place. The fourth time I met Ashmae was when she was writing her first children's book—a celebration of diversity, generosity, and creativity that she hoped to bring to underprivileged and underrepresented children—namely, those who needed it most.

Since these first encounters, I have grown to know Ashmae as an individual, thinker, and seeker. In our frequent email, phone, text, and (when possible) face-to-face conversations, we always seem to come back to our search for and struggle to understand the divine in its various forms: art, nature, relationships, scripture, and our heavenly parents. It was no surprise to me, then, when I read *One Hundred Birds Taught Me to Fly* and found it to be a continued meditation on this theme.

Ashmae's book differs from typical authoritative books about religious scholarship, doctrine, or practice. It reads differently. It speaks differently. It mixes poetry, prose, and art. It eschews an authoritative tone and adopts a markedly personal one. There are no footnotes and there is no bibliography. Even so, *One Hundred Birds* is part of two distinctive and distinguished traditions of religious letters—devotional writing and women's writing. These traditions, which I'll describe in turn, expand and enrich our understanding of religious writing and scholarship.

One way to approach *One Hundred Birds* is as a collection of devotional writing whose heritage predates writing itself. The editors of a recent anthology of devotional poetry called *Before the Door of God* note that *devotion* is regularly associated with the word *colloquy*, signaling that writings in this tradition are conversations with the divine.[1] Such writings "enact the drama of a mind *figuring something out*." As such, they most frequently focus on "religious observance and

---

1. Jay Hopler, "Editor's Preface," in *Before the Door of God: An Anthology of Devotional Poetry*, ed. Jay Hopler and Kimberly Johnson (New Haven: Yale University Press, 2013), xxi.

spiritual questioning," on an individual's efforts to understand their faith, their God, and their place on this earth as well as in heaven.[2] The voice of such works is understandably private and personal. Readers are offered a view into the heart, mind, and soul of one appealing to, reaching for, pleading with, and sometimes railing against God. Early examples of such devotional writing include the Psalms, Job, and Jeremiah. Some of the greatest poets in the English language wrote devotional poetry—John Donne, John Milton, Robert Herrick, George Herbert, Anne Bradstreet, Phillis Wheatley, William Blake, Elizabeth Barrett Browning, Gerard Manley Hopkins, William Butler Yeats, and many more.

Ashmae's work resonates with this tradition in its questioning, exploring, struggling, and beseeching. Throughout the book we read literal stories of seeking—as a convert, missionary, daughter, mother, and artist. She takes us wandering through real places—Uruguay, Norway, Sweden, California, and Utah. These stories are similar to John Bunyan's classic *Pilgrim's Progress*, where the physical landscape is a metaphor for the spiritual landscape in which the writer's soul wanders in search of the divine. At the same time, Ashmae's landscapes offer literal access to the divine. She finds peace, understanding, knowledge, empathy, and the presence of her

---

2. Kimberly Johnson, "'A Heauenly Poesie': The Devotional Lyric," in *Before the Door of God*, ed. Hopler and Johnson, xxix.

heavenly parents in the water, hills, animals, and rocks of this earth, and also in the other people she encounters there.

In this way, her work is reminiscent of three touchstone twentieth-century writers—Annie Dillard, Louise Glück, and Mary Oliver. Similar to Dillard—who wrote in *Holy the Firm*, "I came here to study hard things . . . and to temper my spirit on their edges"—Ashmae traverses climes both physical and metaphysical to wrestle with those hard things that impede, give way to, and constitute the divine.[3] The poetic voice in *One Hundred Birds* seeks for God in both usual and unusual places, acknowledging, like the female gardener in Glück's *Wild Iris*, that God means to teach us how

> to love the world, making it impossible
> to turn away completely, to shut it out completely
>   ever again—
> it is everywhere.

More often than not, the "it" in the world *is* God: "you were left to me."[4] Ashmae uses language in various forms to work out that understanding, as the poet Mary Oliver wrote:

> And what else can we do when the mysteries present
>   themselves

3. Annie Dillard, *Holy the Firm* (New York: Perennial, 1977), 19.
4. Louise Glück, "Vespers," *Wild Iris* (New York: Ecco Press, 1992), 52.

but hope to pluck from the basket the brisk words
that will applaud them.[5]

Similar to other devotional writers, Ashmae uses her words as an exploration, expression, and celebration of faith both lost and found.

In creating this devotional work, she is also participating in a markedly female tradition of Christian writing. Often grouped together under the name "mystics," these early Christian women sought "earnestly and diligently," with "faith, hope, and charity," to understand and express their relationship with the divine.[6] These accounts were most often written in the first person and were deeply—sometimes painfully—personal. While some of their experiences were recorded by male priests and scribes, many of these women adopted a range of noncanonical forms to express their particular need and love for God, Christ, and the feminine divine. These writings were unique because women were routinely denied access to conventional modes of education, print production, and textual transmission. Excluded from church hierarchy and denied the chance to teach or expound from scripture publicly, many female mystics chose writing

5. Mary Oliver, "Mysteries, Four of the Simple Ones," in *New and Selected Poems, Vol. Two* (Boston: Beacon Press, 2005), 9–10.
6. Julian of Norwich, *Revelations of Divine Love* (San Bernardino, CA: First Rate Publishers, 2015), x.

so they might claim their spiritual agency as legitimate and author it for themselves. Consider Hadewijch's poetry, or Hildegard of Bingen's spiritual, medical, and botanical essays, or the more personal accounts of Julian of Norwich, Margery Kempe, and Bridget of Sweden—a diverse collection of women encountering the divine in its many forms.

And this is what we find in *One Hundred Birds*. It is an account of one's search for and encounters with the divine; a record of an individual's desire to feel the love not just of a Heavenly Father, but also of a Heavenly Mother; a celebration of the holiness found in what some might dismiss as small, mundane, or quotidian.[7] Similar to early Christian mystics, Ashmae bears witness to a transcendently divine love that everyone may feel, even as she acknowledges that there are few things we flawed and flailing human beings can know with absolute certainty. She teaches us that even though we might not "know," we can hope with a fervent hope, and in that hope, we can find peace. These underlying themes transcend

7. Latter-day Saint belief in a Mother in Heaven has found expression in official and unofficial settings from the first decades of Mormonism to the present. See David L. Paulsen and Martin Pulido, "'A Mother There': A Survey of Historical Teachings about Mother in Heaven," *BYU Studies* 50/1 (2011): 70–97; Elaine Anderson Cannon, "Mother in Heaven," in *Encyclopedia of Mormonism,* ed. Daniel H. Ludlow, 5 vols. (New York: Macmillan, 1992), 2:961; and the LDS Church's Gospel Topics essay, "Mother in Heaven," https://www.lds.org/topics/mother-in-heaven.

denominational boundaries even as Ashmae employs ideas and terms that may seem peculiar to readers beyond her own tradition, the Church of Jesus Christ of Latter-day Saints.

One Hundred Birds is a witness, a prayer, and a parable—in sharing her "story," Ashmae invites us to examine our own spiritual narrative. This is due in part to her use of a personal voice and the personal *I*. In *One Hundred Birds*, the *I* is Ashmae, but it is also you and me. *I* invites identification, for while we all may be different, we are each an *I*, a being searching for understanding. An *I* is an *eye* that allows us to see ourselves from a different perspective—to re-view our own story of faith, doubt, hope, and salvation. Unlike a third-person narrative that sets up the author as an "expert" and therein distances itself from the reader, the first-person *I* puts us all on equal footing and invites each reader to participate in the book's work of practicing and perfecting faith.

Another way to think of this book's form is as a collection. Indeed, collections and collecting are recurring themes here. Ashmae writes, "As a college student I was a collector of things that I sensed were valuable" (p. 125), whether that was wildflower seeds or women's stories in the Harold B. Lee Library's Special Collections. This book is a collection of collections—fourteen sections that include stories and images on themes like grace, creativity, and laughter. As recipients of this collection, women and men are expected to discover connections among the various pieces. We are invited to locate the similarities and to puzzle through the seeming differences. In that way, our work as readers is reminiscent of another storied LDS creative tradition: quilting. *One Hundred Birds* offers us a collection of pieces and asks us to recognize the beauty in each individual scrap while envisioning a pattern running throughout. We then stitch the pieces together using the fiber of our own lives, creating a unique tapestry together.

Thus, this devotional book *is* a colloquy—a conversation; yet, it is not just a conversation with the divine, but also with all of us as we seek to create heaven here on earth. For even as *One Hundred Birds* is an intimate, quiet, and sometimes raw account of one person's search for God, it is an expansive and inclusive experience. As we identify with Ashmae's *I*, we become part of a *we*. As we make connections between the various sections and types of writing—as we bridge gaps, create points of contact, and see how seemingly different things actually are in conversation—we are practicing the work of building Zion. Ashmae reflects, "I wanted the work of my own salvation to have less to do with me and more to do with what I might offer others" (p. 174), and *One Hundred Birds* offers us many opportunities to reflect on our own journey and to consider ways we might better minister to saints and strangers alike. We are all called to create connections, to envision how our different beliefs and practices—within and beyond our own traditions—might fit together to make something bigger and better than ourselves alone. It is in these moments and places that we find the divine. The work is hard, but in it we find holiness. Through it we create Zion.

—Kristin L. Matthews
Associate Professor of English
Brigham Young Universtiy

LOST

I dreamt I sent my canary son on a bus,
thinking he would know the way home.
But then, the red buses, their numbers dictating
a thousand paths to a thousand mother arms.
My skinny-legged son swinging sweaty
on the blue seats, the silly sailboats and confetti
his fingers trace. When will he know he is lost?
I got to panicking. The rise of the frantic lamb mother bleating.
And then I got to crying and sobbing so my husband woke me.
The lolling Swedish sun ruthlessly sending light into our room at 3:00 a.m.
I just want a little privacy this night, a little darkness to hold me in.
In the morning I told my son about the dream,
and now he tells it as a story, embellished each time.
"Remember, I got lost on the bus, and you cried,
and I told the woman I have a sister and a dog, and she took me home."
Dear woman, I don't know how you found the one bridge
that crosses from Stockholm onto our little island,
but thank you.
Thank you.
We are,
all of us,
foreigners in this land.

Heart

I N THE TEMPLE I put all my senses to work searching for Her. A painting on the wall depicting a woman holding a giggling child in the air above her. The chandelier in the celestial room with the flowers on the table below it. The scent of fresh laundry on my rented temple clothes, and I thought of all the women's hands gathering, washing, folding and distributing. I got tired and rested my chin on my chest while I sat quietly and felt that someone understood. I listened, and listened, and listened through the words that were spoken, through the racing thoughts of my own mind, through my questions; I listened and the quietness spoke back, a quietness that got louder and louder, until as I walked down the stairs back to the dressing room, the words pressed themselves into the palms of my hands and soft places of my heart—"Spread my name like wildfire." When I got to the dressing room, I stood looking at myself in the mirror, my eyes pretty and deep like a still lake beginning to ripple before rain, a strength in them I had never noticed before.

TWELVE TIMES I PRAYED

LYING IN BED. On my knees. Sleeping on my knees. Lost on a bus in Sweden. Head pressed to dark airplane glass on the way to Uruguay. The man in Naples selling candy on the street—I did not buy any but wept later when I thought of his dark, lonely eyes. When I saw my grandma take her last breath, and then I went into the hallway of the nursing home and ate a hamburger with my siblings. At the edge of the dock looking over a frozen lake with my two children. Driving through a canyon on my way to be married in a place my ancestors settled. When my grandfather died ten days after my grandma. Over the phone in my college dorm, I did not say a word to anyone but went to my poetry class and damned all the words that did not come at so precious a time. Knelt down, tying my children's shoelaces, then putting out my palm for the acorn gift. Touch the tops of their rabbit heads.

A T THE BEND where the dirt path met the meadow and
followed a horse pasture with three passive but graceful horses, their wide necks bowed to the wet earth, my two
small children and I felt the sun on our faces for the first
time in days. The horses must have felt the light too. The slow
unshadowing of clouds left arcs of sun across their broad
and speckled bodies. They lifted their heads and treaded the
soft ground, moving nearer us, as if to say, "You feel it too?"
We were far up a path in our rain gear because the showers
showed no signs of slowing when we left the flat on the third
floor just after lunch. We had to get outside though, rainy
or not. The days were too long, slow, and alone with just the
steady beat of the rain to keep our time.

Motherhood can sometimes be so lonely, and not even
in a sad way, just matter-of-fact loneliness, with a hundred
thoughts circling and rarely enough time to properly address
any one of them. I imagine it must feel this way when you
are a child too, and thus is parenting—a few steps across
that shaky bridge between a bigger person and a smaller person, and sometimes a full emboldened sprint to the other

side where we meet each other like perfect and old friends. A fully imperfect attempt to say *we are one because you are my child and I am your parent.* This afternoon of rain, after many afternoons of rain and Carl out of town with fieldwork, even the worms searching for a little refuge on the sidewalks seemed welcome companions.

Remy, Thea, and I moved like wet flowers in our bright rain gear. Up the unfamiliar Swedish road past the white church on the hill where we moved through its graveyard—names I could not pronounce and hardly could fathom the idea that they lived in this place their whole lives. I knew somewhere at the end of the wide expanse of grass and rounded stones was a path to a forest—I just did not know quite where. And so we weaved, making parent and child talk. I was loving my babies and their infinite earnestness so much that day.

IN SWEDISH CEMETERIES they have little stations with watering cans, clippers, and wheelbarrows, and because time was far from the issue, we stopped at one. The rain had let up some. Remy filled the green watering can with the slender spout by pressing his foot to the silver pedal on the ground. He moved deliberately to the flowers at the heads of gravestones and watered them, and I prayed, "Please let my children always find their work in this world." Because by then I'd spent months feeling useless to society and helpless in this new place, I thought the least I could do was perform some meager—and I do mean meager—service. I took the clippers and starting snipping the long grass that had grown up around several of the headstones. It seemed obvious that visitors had long since stopped coming to these particular sites because hiding behind unruly grass was a name, still important somewhere I presume, though long obscured. I do not now remember any of the names I set free with my borrowed clippers, but I let myself believe it was a sort of service to them. A hardly brave but necessary service in one of my humbler hours. Thea tottered, gathering wet grass and clover to her pants.

We moved on through the headstones, and when we got near the outskirts, we saw a gray old man out beyond the gates, the parking spots, the gravel road. At a distance he looked tiny and prim. When we got closer, he was still small and prim but not so gray. He was standing at the crossing of a path and looked as if he were torn between waiting up for this unlikely trio coming through the glum day toward him or heading in another direction, which we later found out to be the headstone of his wife. He opted for us, because it turns out that being a mother is not the only point in life when you can find yourself quite alone.

Like most Swedes, he was terribly polite and spoke perfect English. Remy held up the snail in his palm, and the man said, "That is *snigel* in Swedish"—now numbered among the dozen Swedish words I can recall. A pretty useless word, really, but the fact that someone took the time to teach it to us, to say it over several times until we got it and that Remy held the snail up to his eyes and said *snigel* means I will cherish that word as a passed-on treasure until I am old and forget all my words.

The man, of course, was surprised to find Americans out on his island, much less in a graveyard, in the rain, but he was kind and almost a century old and did not question our running into him here. Our small talk itself felt far more significant to all of us than any of the words actually spoken. He did say my children were beautiful though, and I remember tearing up right on the spot because no stranger says that about your children in Sweden, and all we knew were strangers. We kept walking, turning back to wave a few times until we saw him stop at a spot, and even then he looked up to wave one last time.

In the forest we hiked upward, the path slightly slick with mud but mostly shaded by dense fir trees over us. The rain had turned to a pasty-skied leak, but the light stayed the color of rainy days. I loved to see my children climb over rocks and stop to pick up sticks. It makes me more proud than the act really warrants, but along with the aloneness of parenting, there is no one to limit your pleasure and glee at the mere typical acts of a human being. These moments are yours, because who else is going to delight in their childness? Who else but a parent is going to record each movement on a watching and vulnerable heart?

On we hiked, and Remy kept saying to me, "Mom, I know this place; we are going to the place where there is food." I was confused because this forest looked rather like most forests that Remy, Thea, and I had spent copious amounts of time in. Also, I could not imagine how this faraway path at the edge beyond the graves would lead to food, but he insisted he knew it.

This is the part where we came to the pasture with the horses, the part where the sun finally, and in a sincerely surprising way, came out from the clouds. Didn't just come out, but pushed them all away until we were standing at the one-wired fence, and the horses were moving slowly and curiously toward us, and the sun was beaming on all our eager faces, as if the rain had not been coming down in sheets at lunchtime.

The horses did not ever come near enough for us to pet their noses—they were too wild. But we took our raincoats off and hiked over a hill and into a ravine. The wild blueberries springing up from their low bushes like confetti. The

sunlight coming through the trees like trailing streamers. The spiderwebs, still wet, strung miraculously between tree trunks. The birds making their noises again, filling the forest with sound. To think, just hours before, I had been desolate, desperate, even hopeless inside the quiet flat with my two children.

Remy insisted again that this all felt familiar, and then I recalled Carl had taken them on a hike months before. He had mentioned that it was near the graveyard and that deep into the path, they'd found a little café run by a community of farming people. Remy was right in remembering. And then I stopped and realized that to me, this all felt familiar as well—though in a very different way. This sense of being okay, of being protected and watched over, of helping me know how to take care of my children—it felt like a mother's love. An ancient love that flowered deep inside the furthest recesses of my mind and heart and moved through all of me to that very spot where I stood, and watched my son and my daughter, and I felt that rare gift of being completely understood. Being in this forest felt like remembering, felt like the song of welcoming. Felt like a mother I've always known.

E VEN NOW, as a woman brimming with thoughts, ideas, and experiences, it is difficult to depict myself as the main character of any story. This is slowly, one bold sentence after another, beginning to change. I see already a confidence in my daughter that I am just now unearthing in myself. Once, she got away from me in the foyer during a sacrament meeting and ran straight into the chapel. When I peeked my head in the door, I saw her near the front, marching down the main aisle, her wild curls bouncing, her bare feet, her dress a bright nest of color. I did not move to stop her but instead stood back, watching heads turn to follow her, and felt immensely proud.

FIRST IMPRESSIONS

H E STOOD UP on a picnic table at the family reunion while my husband's youngest sister stood on the ground below, surprised that the announcement was happening now, and in this way. "She's pregnant, and we're getting married." He gestured down toward her with both hands. We reacted to the abruptness with some flustered and quiet clapping, and we eked out our congratulations. My sister-in-law had already run to her cabin, embarrassed by this fiancé we'd met the night before. I didn't like him, and I'm sure he didn't like me.

Also. The man at the doughnut shop who told me he needed a dollar to ride the bus. I went back to my car to rummage, and when I returned to offer up my wrinkled bill, he was already accepting another from someone else. In line with my children while they picked out pink and sprinkles and chocolate please, I saw the man in line. I watched him drinking coffee from a glazed mug, then eating a doughnut, then sitting down and pulling a hot croissant egg-and-sausage sandwich (far too expensive for me) from a greasy white bag, and as I finished the last crumbs of my breakfast, he sipped on fresh orange juice. I looked out the window and realized there was no bus stop anywhere close.

16

My mother's stepmom, who died of intoxication with a neighbor in her trailer a few years after my grandpa died of a heart attack. She took my mom's childhood photographs, the few relics she had of her real mother. She watched a lot of *The Price Is Right*, and my mom claimed she moved out of the house at seventeen to get away from her.

Or the man who was my husband Carl's stepfather for a short time during Carl's teen years. He once pushed Carl into the harbor because he knew he could not swim and thought it might teach him to not be so afraid. He raged drunkenly in the garage, and the darkness of it wafted up into the kitchen and under covers of rumpled beds. He is since no part of anything tangible we know, except in conversation where he recedes even further into the dislike of our memory.

I AM LOOKING TO LOVE BETTER, and I believe there is a mother's heart eager to teach me.

SECOND IMPRESSIONS

THE WAY I SAW the fiancé of my sister-in-law pick up a piece of ember that had escaped the fire with his bare hands and quietly toss it back into the fire because he did not want the kids playing nearby to step on it.

Also. The way the man who asked for my dollar at the doughnut shop was in no hurry, at peace with the world in which he drifted.

And my stepgrandmother—the memories I have of her aren't actually unpleasant at all, though I do not doubt my own mother's sadness. She called me "honey" and pulled me in close to her jelly-roll chest. We spent Thanksgiving with them once at the local high school, and she introduced us to everyone, beaming that we would come all the way to be with her and my grandpa.

After his former stepfather had come by the house in a huff to pick up Carl's half brother, Carl told me about how that grumpy, inexperienced man, thrown so quickly into the fatherhood of five stepchildren and one of his own, spent every weekend for months restoring an old car and teaching Carl the intricacies of his work so Carl wouldn't have to walk the few miles to high school every morning.

A T MY FIFTH-GRADE maturation program, my sweaty kid knees against the metal folding chair, my mom reached over and took my hand. I felt stricken with embarrassment as a delighted volunteer mother held two ripe and reddened grapefruit to her chest and joked about the breasts we would have one day. I wanted to shrink into the orange carpet of the library floor at the talk of blood and bodies, the old VHS tape whirring in the VCR, my mom holding my limp hand in her lap. I did not want to become a woman. No one had ever explained to me much about womanhood, and I equated the call with things that scared me and things I did not want. No one told me that my body was a brilliant temple, that although it might be capable of creating life, it was certainly capable of creating important thoughts and ideas and change. I can only guess no one had ever told my own mother those things either, even after she had accomplished them all.

I prayed I would never start my period, and when I did I felt so betrayed that I cried so hard and so long that my mom did not send me to school, but instead sat with me a long time at the edge of her bed—she in just a towel, still wet from the shower.

My mom's own mother died when she was just fifteen,

and because I am the oldest, my mom and I spent our first thirty years together, setting out like stalwart pioneers as we attempted to navigate the landscape of a mother-daughter relationship. We had no examples to model ourselves after, no lessons or manuals to teach us how to be mother and daughter.

My mom and I got on well for thirty years, with overflowing amounts of love and kindness exchanged, but it was not until a recent snapping cold winter day when I saw her unloading the car on the driveway after a day of work at the hospital as a nurse that something changed. I'd been keeping a notebook of times I felt Heavenly Mother, of things she might want to tell me, of ways I might better know her. I did not expect her, however, to illuminate my own mother in such a way that as I watched her load the groceries, a few bags in each arm, and as I ran down the steps to help her, she was strong and glorious in a way I had not noticed before.

I wanted to go back and help that fifth-grade girl hold her mother's hand firmly in an unspoken pact that promised we would work harder to learn from a Heavenly Mother as well as a Heavenly Father so we could know better how to love each other.

Together/Forever

I CARRY A POCKETFUL of stories about my dad. As a child he stuck his mother's straight pins in every banana of the backyard banana tree. He once pinched my grandpa in the bottom with a pair of pliers because he just could not resist something so funny. I've heard the story a dozen times about the time he was surfing, stayed out too late and too far, and got caught in a terrible riptide against the cliffs at dusk. I revel every time he gets to the part where he thought he was done for, too weak to keep swimming, but he reached his hand up against all odds, and someone pulled him onto the shore. At nineteen, his parents were still holding out hope that he might turn in his mission papers, but he made art, lived in a tent in the mountains, and worked on boats as a deckhand instead. He came home for Sunday dinners, and my grandparents loved him without reservation.

When I was five, Mormon missionaries came to our house, and again when I was six and then seven. One of the images I hold dear from my childhood is my dad, after work, smoking just one cigarette on the back patio while I sat on the stoop near him. Somehow I sensed even then during one of his last patio smokes that he was sacrificing part of his wild self for something he thought would be good for me. He baptized my mom a year later. In the photo he is clean-shaven and trim, his dark eyes illuminate thirty-six years and a hope for many good things. My proud little arms around his neck as he holds me in his white jumpsuit. My dad, a complicated, stubborn, gentle man with a knack for always coming around and doing the right thing—a surprising bouquet of flowers for my mom, kneeling tenderly next to grandkids teaching them how to fish, removing the pins from the banana tree one by one. And what a strange world, when I count my memories backward and land at one, it is his imperfect face I remember first in this world. Blurry, looking down, saying my name.

SEALED

HAVE I EVER encountered kinder women than the ones that watched over my brother, sister, and me in the Provo Temple before we were ushered in to join my parents in the sealing room? I may have met kinder women, my mother-in-law for example, but my child heart saw those women in white as my own personal angels, and still I picture them, floating along the pastel quiet halls of that white building, guiding children by touching them gently on shoulders. A lot of talk from my aunts and grandma about the white

dress I would wear—I mostly can picture that too, the way it poofed nearly all the way to the ground, and I felt nothing short of majestic.

I had no idea then that the whole family had been waiting for my parents. Waiting for my dad to become active again since two decades previous when he made his final stand as a teenager after the Boy Scout leader insisted he wear the whole uniform one week too many. And my mom—my dad's sisters and parents all just loved her so much, and they were elated to see her dressed in white at her baptism and now here in the temple. We left the room scattered with toys feeling some reluctance, but the peacefulness of the walk to the smaller and warmly lit room still accompanies me on rare occasion. The light, the way it made everything feel holy and twinkling, the only sound the shuffle of our socked feet on the padded carpet. Everything was so quiet when we walked through the door, sneaking glances of our never-ending selves in the mirrors on either side of the room. My brother, sister, and I were ushered ever so softly by the women. I saw that everyone was putting tissues to their eyes, and my parents, in the middle kneeling down, put their hands out to us and we walked forward, all eyes on our family.

I N THE BEGINNING, the stories are all about me, with guest appearances of best friends, missionaries, school teachers, God, Jesus, my parents, my grandparents, and always, always, my beloved little brother and sandy-haired little sisters, because who else was there in this world?

Our story is always growing. As we got older, I learned to make macaroni and cheese while my mom was at work in the afternoons. I felt only a bit more capable than I actually was. In Utah for the third grade, everyone had already learned to write in cursive, and I stayed in my desk and cried during recess because I was so humiliated to be different.

My mom worked at the hospital in the catering department, and again, I did not tell a soul because no one else had a mother who worked, and I knew it made my dad sad that she had to. That summer as I babysat my brother and sister, my parents called nearly every hour to check on us. We kept busy, sweeping the deck, playing the old piano in the basement, recording our own talk shows on the tape recorder One afternoon a storm blew in, and we stood at the front window watching the trees sway back and forth.

Ask any kid from that third-grade class now, and surely they would recall "the great Utah microburst of 1994." The

sky darkened, and we scampered around making sure windows were shut. We turned on a show and waited out the stomp of heavy rain and the whisking winds that moved and scraped our patio furniture across the deck. When the winds died down, we opened the screen door and walked out on the wet front lawn to discover a gaping hole and our old oak on its side, the roots torn and clawing the swollen gray sky. My parents called again to make sure we were all right, and the next thing I remember is the tree gone; new grass growing over the once deep scoop of earth that had been lifted; my brother, sister, and I making a tiny mud home in the backyard; and my parents introducing us to a new little sister in daffodil.

SEALING

AFTER TWO DECADES I sat in the same temple room; this time no eyes were on me but on my littlest, beloved, sister who was born after we had been sealed, kneeling across from her new husband at an altar in the room's center. All was graceful. Their relationship was orchestrated in envelopes that made their way across continents while my sister was a missionary in Argentina. We were all in love with the two of them. The twinkling light of the quiet temple rooms had not faded. I sat so I could see into the mirrors on either side of the room, carrying a thousand reflections in either way. A pain started to rise into my throat, and I held back tears as I looked into that mirror and did not see the reflections of two of my siblings next to me.

My brother and sister were watching my children downstairs in the small waiting room. My pain had nothing to do with the reasons they were not there, just simply that they were not. My sister's husband was also missing people in the reflection—his father who died a decade before and his mother who died when he was a small child. I don't know how the absence of my new brother-in-law's parents on his wedding day must have felt, but I have watched him again and again plant seeds of his loss in a wide field of hope. I have watched him sow with tender thoughtfulness. I have watched him gather resplendent bouquets of joy and hope as his flowers grow. He offers bouquets as gifts to everyone around him without stipulation. In some way, in the temple that day, the borders of loss and reunion blurred. People missed each other in very different ways for different reasons during the ceremony, but I believe one day I will better understand the unseen ways in which my sister and her husband were also celebrated.

Later that day, at the wedding lunch, we stood in turn and shared a favorite memory, and many of us cried out of pure joy and celebration. Maybe then, if I had spent more time in the temple that day looking carefully into those mirrors, I would not have seen absences, but the figures of all those memories and stories that make up our lives. I may not have seen my siblings standing next to me in the present, momentary frame, but they would have surrounded us both a thousand frames backward and forward—their absence in that room was not hopeless for me.

History has shown that religion can play the role of divider, but maybe it does not have to. I wanted my siblings to know that while the present moment in the temple mattered immensely, and it was beautiful, that the thousands of moments before—when my sister helped my marrying sister to do her hair that morning, the time we spent at our kitchen table together, the hour we spent in the temple two decades prior being sealed as a family, and then the thousands of hours that will still come as we continue to grow up together—those moments matter. Together they make up the sacred writ of my life. Those many vibrant hours are what I saw in temple mirrors that day. I want to tell my brother and sister that I saw them there, that when I looked into the mirrors I was not alone at all, that I saw us all going behind me and in front of me together for as far as I could see.

I DO NOT KNOW much about my mom's mother. She died when my mom was fifteen, and my mom said her father cried so loudly as the elevator descended to the bottom floor of the hospital that the nurses must have wept right along with him. I do not know what those next days or even years looked like except that so much of my mom's life after that moment is marked by her motherlessness.

For my whole life an oil painting of a field and a stone bridge crossing into a lit cottage has hung above my mom's bed. Her mother painted it, and Mom adorned it with a garish gold frame that does not match anything else in our house. Even as a kid I would stand on the pillows and run my fingers over the thick brushstrokes, hoping to understand a little about the woman who left my own mom wanting so desperately for more. When I was a teenager, my aunt mentioned to my mom that I had inherited their mother's big bosom, and I had no idea what to make of the comment, unsure of whether to be proud or embarrassed.

A photograph of her stands in a silver frame on my mom's dresser, and I cannot figure out much of how she must have been, except that her smile is not pretend, and her absence has changed all our lives. When I was a teenager, I urged

my mom to do her mother's temple work after my grandpa had also passed away. I do not remember many details about the actual day, what happened before or after our time in the temple, but I do recall sitting in the small office off the baptismal font where the confirmation blessings are given. The ordinance was short, performed by men who also maybe knew something of loss, ushered in and out of doors by women who may have had daughters of their own. The power in that moment as my mom cried unquietly felt transcendent. With hands on my mom's head, the men offered the blessing for her mother, and I sensed something of this grandmother I did not know. More than anything, I sensed she loved my own mom dearly. Something about our experience in the temple that morning offered a kind of hope nothing else could give my mom.

We haven't spoken of the day since, but now when I go home and see the painting above the bed, I picture my mom crossing that stone bridge, over the meager stream, and into that cottage, where surely, a warm meal must be ready and waiting, a clean bed with the sheets turned down, a long-awaited embrace as the sun outside begins to set.

I HAVE ALWAYS ADORED my younger brother, Dane, as if there were some unreasonable forging of our two very different souls sometime long before we came to my parents. We hardly understand each other, except in that space where I call him brother and he calls me sister, and then, understanding is as deep and strong as the roots of an aspen grove.

At my sister's wedding lunch, I overhead him tell a story to an old mission companion that none of us had ever heard. He talked about a giant of a companion he once had, a boy that went on to play college football and who loved my brother dearly. As missionaries, there was a misunderstanding one night about who was to teach a lesson at an investigator's house, and unbeknownst to my brother, the companion had become quietly furious. By the time they got home and shut the apartment door, Dane told his companion, "You seem upset. I'm sorry—I'm not sure what is wrong, but do what you need to do." To his surprise, this towering teddy bear reared back and punched him right in the face, knocking him down. Dane stood up calmly, and the companion punched him one more time, and then he was done. They both felt terrible, but Dane left it at that and went to bed.

As Dane recounted the story, which was the first we had

ever heard of it, several guys who had known him as a missionary could hardly believe what they were hearing. Dane said he knew this boy would be sent home if he ever told anyone then. Even when the mission president asked directly if there were problems, he said nothing. After he finished telling the story, he sat back and laughed in the comfortable way he always has when something is slightly absurd.

In between the time he came home from his mission and the time he recounted this story, there were a few years that this same heroic brother was in a place so far beyond my reaching that I could do nothing but wake up crying to nightmares when I thought I'd lost him forever. Drug addiction rendered him nearly unrecognizable for a time, except for the familiar way he always spoke about God as if there were never any doubt he was loved immeasurably. His faith in godly love during those years shocked me because a lot of things in his life did not line up with happiness. Yet, at his lowest points, he spoke of God's love and how through it he would get over his addiction and get his life back, and sometimes no one else believed him, except probably him and God.

I should not be surprised though at Dane's propensity to give love and his constant disposition to receive it. His willingness to be enfolded by the love of God, even in his darkest hours, and the ability to offer it to someone else in their pain has saved not only him, but others around him. A bit of grace like an unexpected gift, my brother, over and over.

M Y SISTER SAGE stopped attending church nearly a decade ago. She moved away slowly, almost imperceptibly, after the disappointment of passing on the sacrament trays without being able to lift anything to her lips for too many Sundays left her feeling hopeless and rebellious.

Growing up, my sister was always next to me on the chapel pew in dresses that would not allow her entrance to a stake dance, but she was there. And though we rarely talked about the things that moved us in our church experience, I often looked over to see tears welling the corners of her eyes when someone spoke of Jesus and the love of God.

She battled anorexia, experimented with drugs, and had a boyfriend who coerced her into skipping classes and wouldn't allow her to attend seminary. At the time, my family only partly knew this story, and certainly we were not prepared to tell it to anyone. My own inability to confront difficult things I had never faced myself made me a sister with good intentions, but one who could hardly understand my sibling, let alone save her.

Years later in my living room one night after our children had fallen asleep upstairs—chubby, hopeful cousin hands held in the dark—we entered the realm of conversation that is as textured with memory as it is honesty. As I sat and listened to my sister just younger than me unfold years of her life in sentences I had never heard her speak, I was moved by her candidness and heavyhearted at the anger I suspected she had long harbored. She resented bishops whose words, though well-intentioned, filled her delicate teenage heart with guilt and shame. She talked about the bishop who did not bring the temple recommend of her boyfriend—now husband—on the temple tour for the youth, even though they had stopped kissing altogether in order to be considered worthy to worship at the temple. My heart ached as she described that young boy sitting in the foyer, head down, waiting for the rest of the group to finish.

When they were young, pregnant, getting married, and had no intention of coming back to church, the bishop performing the ceremony spoke of their eventual sealing in the temple, of Joseph Smith, of the Book of Mormon. My sister, full with baby and trying to be brave, hurt deeply at the reminder in that moment of all the things she still was not, standing before family and our neighborhood on her wedding day.

Later as a missionary, I could sense the weight of hurt behind the blessed offering of support in letters she wrote me, and the same again when she waited outside the temple on my wedding day and when she came to my childrens' blessing days and her husband could not join in the circle.

As a teenager growing up in the heart of Mormon culture, I worried that my sister would never find any peace

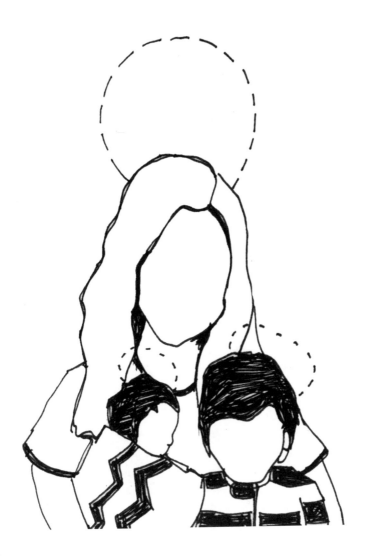

the further she diverged from the familiar path laid out by the church. I worried for her in the same way I worried for the girl from my high school whose parents drank wine. I am embarrassed now to think that I ever questioned the happiness of another because it did not match perfectly my own, but my young heart was not ready to understand that the thread between my sister and me would not even waver, let alone break, in the years to follow, even when our lives looked different.

She was lost for a time, but I do not believe that for a second God lost her. I believe she was carried—just as I was, and my brother, and my other sister, and my mom and dad—by heavenly parents in the soft way one might care for a slight bird. They carried her, a tender weight in palm, until she was ready and able to again fly and find happiness in her life even beyond the church we grew up in together. And they carried me as I tried to make sense of so much change in the lives of people I love.

For too long I did not know that my sister had been writing her own spiritual narrative in the place beyond her Mormon upbringing. Too often I had been so intent on helping her reclaim and fix the old one that I did not stop to consider that she was continuing to do new and exciting work on her own story. She had been writing all along, though. She had taken responsibility for both the hard things and the good things her spiritual life had given her from the beginning. A different story than mine, yes. Traversing the breadths of doubt and joy like mine, yes. Still rooted in many concepts and ideas we learned together in those sacrament pews, yes. In talking to her, I believe we still pray to the same kind God.

As we talked that night, I thought of her little boys sleeping next to Remy and Thea in their beds upstairs—their absolute delight at spending time together. I thought of the ways their tiny lives were starting to weave stories that, from the outset, would uniquely play out. Then I remembered earlier that afternoon in a forest full of cocooning caterpillars and light shining through bright green trees as we all hiked together, two generations wandering through the unknown. There were no rules dictating the way we could feel awe; there was no insistence that each had to be an active church member to feel the way that God loves us all—we felt that love in the space not where religion meets religion, but in the space where our stories unfold to each other.

My sister has a story she also wants to tell. One that I want to hear.

I wish I had told her sooner.

O NCE WHEN WE WERE LIVING in Sweden, my family came across a dozen fawns grazing in a meadow. The sun sat low in an evening sky that we sensed would never grow dark, and we stopped and watched these slender animals, their bright black eyes flicking quietly, the white spots on their backs like swaths of cream. They did not move upon hearing my children, husband, and me as we rustled through blueberry bushes and crunched the dry sticks on the ground with our slow-moving feet. They continued bending their heads to the ground, as if communing in steadfast prayer between looking up at us and lowering again.

When I think of them now, I think of my littlest sister, Bayley. I think of her tender beaming belief in the world's essential goodness. I think of the way she trusted me, her older sister of ten years, when she crashed on her bike while I was babysitting; before we bandaged her knees while she sat at the kitchen counter, she stopped crying long enough to let me pray with her. I must have been about sixteen. I cannot exactly remember why I thought to pray, except that I must have believed it would teach her something about the way prayers are answered. She remembers that moment still, though neither of us can recall the specific outcome or the

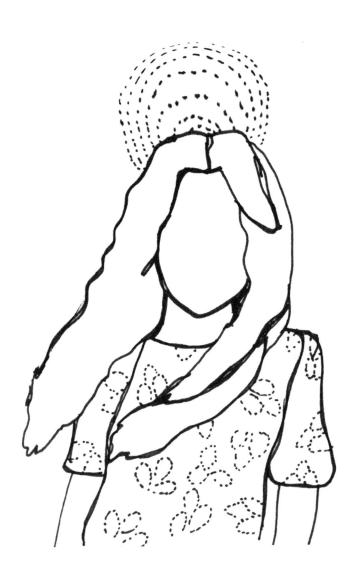

surrounding events—just that we prayed there together as sisters.

I still sometimes want to bring her that close and with a bit more wisdom acquired over another decade tell her that doubts will come and questions will interrupt. But because they can also enrich she needs not fear them. I want to tell her I've experienced my own pain and the pain of others as I've unfolded my own spiritual story, and that she too should prepare for hurt—it is not the end. I want to assure her I have also found bountiful joy in keeping promises and in making sacrifices for what I believe to be good. I want to impart to her strength in the face of struggles she might face, and I want to tell her to come to me when they appear.

But something wiser tells me to wait, to be quiet. My sister is intelligent and perceptive and full of belief yet unstirred by the turbulence of doubt. The pictures from her mission in Argentina where she stands with families in white on their baptism day glow with an unearthly light. Her wedding day in the temple was marked by joy in what was to come, by comfort in covenant, by eagerness in obedience. It is not mine to tell my sister the way her life will fill with both sting and exuberance, sometimes more of one than the other, because she will know whom to go to for both thanksgiving and restitution. I only need to love her faith. She is a quiet fawn in a light-filled meadow, impervious to the noise of the world, bowing her beautiful head again and again in unadorned and experienced prayer.

M Y HUSBAND CARL says his earliest and best memory is the Easter with his three older siblings when they lived in a trailer at the end of an undeveloped road in north-ernmost California. Each night leading up to Easter, his mom would look into their ears and pretend one at a time to pull jelly beans out of nowhere. He says he remembers they were the cheap crystalline kind with a thick shell of sugar. A world that could have been so harsh to him was kind in his mother's keeping.

A few years later and in a new state, a kind man from the local ward had begun to drop by Carl's home weekly with filled cardboard boxes from the grocery store where he worked, and the expired food kept dinner on the table.

Beginning after the great flood of 1996, when Carl was ten, he said for weeks afterwards they found their toys out in the fields that lay adjacent to their solitary house in the country, plastic arms sticking up out of the mud, and they huddled together without electricity in the upstairs room, their father, the strongest man alive, heaving all the soggy furniture out of the upstairs open window. Beginning then,

Carl marks a before and an after, a quick coming of age, of realizing that the world both is and is not perfect.

At age twelve, after his parent's divorce, Carl began to attend church alone while his siblings stayed behind and his mom worked the night shift at the hospital. His dad, now back in California, was building fences and sleeping in storage units.

Stubborn and unwilling to leave that shamble of a town when his mom moved the family into the city to be closer to work, Carl and his brother opted to finish out the school year in a friend's house, also flooded yet never repaired. When school ended, they boarded a greyhound bus to work with their dad for the summer. His dad, clean and kind, had asked the temple receptionist if he and his sons could sleep in the parking lot for a few days when they arrived. He felt it a more proper welcoming, a place they'd feel safe.

Carl says he'll never forget waking up those mornings to Moroni's golden trumpet and the beaming face of his Dad who had slept in the back of the truck so Carl could have the cushioned cab.

At age fourteen, after a move to the city, Carl continued to go to church, and the young men's group began to change the kind of activities they did on Wednesday nights—a skate park, a hike through a creek, a listen to the latest punk rock albums. Carl, sometimes only showing up because a leader drove to get him, did not realize that no one else in his group was into skateboarding and punk rock albums until years later when he stopped to think about the kindnesses we cannot recognize when we are young.

When Carl was sixteen, an older man from the ward came to pick him up once a month to visit families in the ward that no longer came to church. The man would bring a baseball hat for Carl to wear over his blue hair. Once when Carl had forgotten about the appointments, the man drove across town to Carl's friend's house where they were playing video games. He was not angry or impatient with him—he just told him they'd made a commitment, and it was time to go. Carl speaks of that act as something that changed him.

It was in these houses, sitting at dinner tables and around couches, that my husband began to believe that maybe he could graduate from high school and maybe go on to college.

Before Carl left on his mission, his mother began to come back to church on Sunday mornings after her night shift, sitting in the back folding chairs, hoping no one would notice her tired mother eyes or nursing scrubs—this was the beginning of a different kind of life for her, one in which she began to see herself in the kind and capable ways that perhaps only her own mother had long seen her.

During his freshman year of college, Carl walked out of his last test and saw his final score—he had passed his first year with perfect marks, something his teenage self who barely graduated from high school was incapable of envisioning. Out in the snow he cried with gratitude the whole walk home. This beginning was composed of a thousand fragments of doubt, depression, disbelief in his ability or worth that dissipated and reformed into the belief that he was capable, that indeed he had been watched over all along.

Grace

I N A SMALL TOWN in Uruguay on the border of Brazil, we spent most of our time in the neighborhood at the top of a large hill. We found dead chickens on the stone street once, and it was rumored that black magic had happened the night before. We met a young mother there who had a son who could not walk or talk. She carried him everywhere with her tiny frame, and we were there in her one-room house watching her sit on the bed looking at him in the morning light, and my heart broke open as I understood a little more about the possibility for unselfishness we all possess. A Brazilian grandmother in the house on a corner was always halfway out the front window dancing to samba at dusk—she felt like a symbol of joy. On Easter all the children built kites out of sticks and tissue paper, and we sat on a front lawn watching them all rising into the sky, colored and cobbled out of the simplest things their world could afford them—one hundred birds teaching me to fly.

A STRAWBERRY PICKER by day and wife to a drunk by night, Blanca nodded with conviction, even when we taught her about tithing. She cooked us fatty meat and greasy rice in the makeshift kitchen tent that swayed in front of the garden and then sent us inside to sit in the only room in the house to eat while the family waited out back. The garden stretched so far out we could barely see the ends of the rows, and in the summer the fat toads croaked into the breathless heat of dusk. I was twenty-one, and at the edge of this garden, dinosaur chickens pecking mindlessly and the Uruguayan sunsets stretching taut around us like a colorful quilt. The whole world felt new to me. You could toss a seed into the soil, and it would grow within the month. Blanca grew things almost as well as she cultivated the most honest faith I've ever encountered. I cannot forget the way the dirt etched permanently into the deep cracks on her hands. I saw her wash them, scrub them, but still, when she handed us our bowls of rice or turned the wispy pages of the scriptures, I saw the rich, black bits of earth did not leave her.

She walked the dusty road to church each Sunday and married the man she had lived with for twenty-five years. She prayed and stumbled through scriptures, gleaning and harvesting as if there were nothing else in the world that might offer her sustenance. By day she patiently toiled with the soil, weeds, plants, and food that eventually came, and by night, she treated the scriptures in the same gentle, patient way, as if she were walking among the passages stooping to glean and her life depended on the harvest. A couple of people came when she was baptized. I once asked a missionary who served in the same neighborhood a few years later if Blanca still walked to church every Sunday, but he said he had never seen her. The last thing I remember Blanca telling me was this: "I was picking strawberries, and I was praying and praying. I reached my hand in to pull off a strawberry, and there was a snake hiding inside the bush. I wasn't scared because I knew God was with me."

CARLOS COMING UP THE ROAD on his rusty bicycle, his dirt-crusted boots pumping the pedals and his long, spindly legs turning like pieces of wire. If he had been drinking, he glared and slurred curse words at us, and mostly we were embarrassed for him. He had set off down the long rows of the garden, stooping to finger the cilantro, the chickens surrounding him, curious as if they'd never seen a drunk man. One afternoon while we taught Blanca in

the bedroom, he stood outside near the well and pounded on the wall with both fists. Blanca, who hardly raised her voice above a whisper, excused herself and went out back. Through the wall we heard her yell at him like thunder raised from her belly. She sent him away, and then we saw him idle into the field through the faded daisies on the thin, falling curtain, like a young boy with shoulders drooping. When she came back in, we started at the same word we had left off in the scriptures. I glimpsed conviction in a way my life had never required of me. We walked down the highway at dusk, and I pictured Blanca praying, not just for herself, but for the life of Carlos, and for us, in all our smallness.

IN ORDER TO BE BAPTIZED, Blanca and Carlos had to be married because they had lived together for twenty-five years. The first time, we rode buses to the county building—Blanca in crisp, black pants and combed hair, parted down the middle and pulled back. She did not say much on the way there, or when Carlos did not show up because he had gotten too drunk at work, or on the way home when we bumped along on the old bus seats, back to the garden and the one-room house on the side of the freeway. When Blanca got out, we waved and said we would try again soon.

A new appointment at the clerk's office, a saved-up payment of $25, and a sober Carlos, and they were married. Although I've looked back on this scenario with guilt and worry at what we'd actually done for Blanca. Had we just made her life more difficult in our quest for righteous living? I do remember that evening when the sun was down and we gathered at the shifty wooden table outside the kitchen tent. Sons and daughters I did not even know existed showed up, and grandkids ran through the field. There was a cake, so big it filled the table. The white meringue was glossy and stood stiff and wondrous. Someone pretended to know how to play a ukulele, and we all sang. Carlos beamed and put his arm around Blanca and pulled her close. For those minutes he was beautiful.

Even still, a decade later, I imagine his liver is nearly failing from the alcohol he never stopped drinking, or it has already killed him. I imagine he is a little bit horrible, perhaps even a despicable character, but the way I saw him beam that night, the way he cut the cake in large pieces and handed them out to everyone, even the grandkids, there is something in that moment that tells me there are heavenly parents and we are sailing more swiftly to their arms than we have any idea of.

Rosa, who lived down the road from Blanca, reminded me of a turtle. She had put in her teeth, which did not seem to fit very well, when we came to the door. She sat in her big wooden chair and watched out the window at Susana the lamb, who would be eaten for Christmas dinner. One day when we came I put a butterfly sticker in the corner of her window to remind her to be happy. She told us that every morning and every night she talked to the little butterfly. Rosa could not read, never learned how, and I wondered what this world is without words. We, of course, did not try very hard then to get her to the church to baptize her. For one, the problem of reading and understanding. If the point of baptism is to become as a little child, she was already there. The other problem was her feet, like two potatoes stuffed on the end of her puffy brown legs. She hardly walked at all, except when her husband Freites heaved her from behind up to the dinner table and back again into her wooden rocking chair. I got to feeling sorry for her, until as we were making her bed one morning, I saw a photograph in a cheap silver frame propped on the nightstand. It was Rosa and her husband dancing. Rosa, younger, but still in a flour-sack dress and short, wild hair. Her husband, Freites, a bicycle repairer, without a shirt or shoes. The way they held each other in the photo made me believe that this is the joy the world had to offer them. Not words, not even a whiff of wealth, not vast comprehension or formal religion, but a small butterfly sticker on a dirty window, a lamb, a wooden chair, a warm body in the bed at night, someone to sit across the table and eat soup with. This world's offerings were enough for them.

CARLA, WHO WAS BAPTIZED just before I arrived in her area, had a promiscuous mother who brought home nonchalant boyfriends and two aunts who swept the dirt from the kitchen with a homemade broom. The house smelled dark and of stale cooking oil.

One night when we came for a visit, Carla led us through the tunnel of a hallway to a room scraped together with the detritus of the neighborhood. Suffocating, dilapidated ceilings; the tiny window carved through the corrugated metal and covered by a striped cloth; the bed, damp and made of an old mattress balanced atop a wooden crate, balanced atop some mud bricks; and crumbling cardboard boxes of clothes shoved in corners.

Everything was made from something that had long worn out its purpose, except her Book of Mormon, laid carefully on the shelf beside her bed. I was surprised and embarrassed at my own timidity around real poverty, as if this level of poor had a life and personality that recognized my uselessness. No heat, no electricity, no privacy from the wild screams of her three younger brothers and the shrill voice of one of the aunts with futile attempts to control them. We pulled out a flash-light and read some scriptures.

Carla was pretty, but plump with malnourishment. She went to church every Sunday, sometimes still with poverty following her in the shadows so that she made faces at the pretty girls who did not live in houses with dirt floors. The bishop sent her home with food, and the family descended on the spoils. For a teenager, Carla understood so well, and more deeply than she ever let on. In my six months living around the corner from her, I watched Carla dive to the depths of an-ger in waters far too deep for her and by some divine miracle, surface on the beach of hope a hundred times.

The one winter I lived in her town, her family invited my companion and me for Christmas dinner. When we walked around the side of the house, white lights were strung from the trees, and a table was laid out with a tablecloth and an assortment of borrowed cups and plates. Bowls of meat and rice, lentils and fresh loaves of bread, cake, meringue, and cheap soda crowded the table. The whole family—combed and in their nicest clothes, and the boys for once behaving—

sat waiting for us. Because missionaries are always the first to be invited for dinner in a poor, foreign place, we'd already eaten three Christmas meals, and my guilt at feeling full nearly made me weep. But that day—years before I would write to Carla and learn that she was pregnant, and her little sister Diana, still a teen, was pregnant, and both the aunts had died, and her mother had left with a boyfriend, and the boys were old enough to take care of themselves—that day, I sat up to the table, we held hands and prayed, and then we feasted as if none of us had ever eaten a Christmas meal before in our lives.

ON MY FIRST DAY out in the field as a missionary, I breathed in every detail my area had to offer. The grocery store that played a "Police" song, the cereal I bought that tasted like chocolate-covered Styrofoam, the slight rocky hill that led from our apartment down to the water where we could see the lights of Buenos Aires, the way the sky seemed to be larger than the earth, like we were on a tiny island of land in the middle of a sea of sky. I trotted alongside my lanky, blond companion with the grandest visions any missionary may have ever had, when she turned to me and said, "It's okay, I guess you don't bug me that bad." Fair enough.

She studied Isaiah exclusively during companionship study, and although I understood little Spanish those first weeks, I got the impression sitting next to her in the homes of very poor people that Isaiah was not the lesson material they were connecting to. We made a rule that we had to leave the house on time in the mornings so sometimes she headed out to teach our investigators and make street contacts with just one eye of elaborate makeup done and the other plain as could be. Once we made a giant pot of soup for a woman down the street, and the woman was so confused when we brought it to her front door she turned us away. One afternoon my companion had a nervous breakdown after rubbing her eye with jalapeno still on her finger; I did not know what to do, so I called the elders from the next town over and waited by the front door while she screamed and cried. I loved her so much, though I did not know how to touch her sadness, and that was my loss.

On her last Sunday in the ward she surprised me and everyone else in the small branch by walking to the front of the chapel, towering over the rickety pulpit and wobbly microphone and singing a cappella all four verses of "I Know That My Redeemer Lives." I was shocked, embarrassed, totally intrigued, and by the time she was done, completely moved by her bravery. Not so much to belt that song in a land not her own, in a language secondary to her native English, but because she did it despite everything: her brother in jail, her parents' divorce, the rumors about her I later found circulating throughout the mission, the members who did not like her. She sang about a belief in Christ despite her own failings and the many things that had failed her.

VANESSA AND GABRIEL lived in a one-room house with tall ceilings and so many spiders lazily living in unreachable corners of the tall ceiling. They cooked polenta on a brick Gabriel had wrapped with wire. They washed their clothes in a big red bucket and shared a tin outhouse with the neighbors. They felt like pure joy to us. Gabriel told the best jokes and brought me back a whole roll of stickers from the orange factory he worked at. To this day, when I think of the prettiest person I've ever known, I think of Vanessa, breastfeeding her baby girl, the baby's older sister toddling nearby under the tree while we all read the Book of Mormon, talking our way through each verse. I think of Gabriel strumming his guitar to Primary songs while we all sang along.

Vanessa and Gabriel had been married and baptized just weeks before I arrived in their area, and to be privy to their enthusiasm to do the right things in those first months of their church membership was humbling. I find that too often

I am skeptical to act before I have all the reasons why. I want to say that I know better, as though religion must be a metaphor for something bigger, but then I think back on Vanessa and Gabriel and how when the missionaries first met them they were not married but had been together for many years and had two children. As the lessons progressed, the missionaries got to the law of chastity. My companion, who was there, said that because they did not know how to address the particular situation, they simply taught the church's law of chastity prohibiting sex before marriage and left it at that. A few months later, because it takes time to process paperwork, Vanessa and Gabriel were married, their two baby girls squirming in their few wedding photos taken with a snap-and-shoot camera.

Not until weeks later, when I arrived at the area, did they tell us that while they had shared a bed for those three months previous to their marriage, they had not had sex once because they wanted to be obedient to the law of chastity. The part of me that is proud wants to believe in exceptions to rules, for a God who surely must understand that there was a way around for them, but then I think again about the way Vanessa and Gabriel were not sad or resentful about their decision, but confident and grateful and sure of the blessings that had come because of their sacrifice.

Years later I still wrestle with the letter-of-the-law-type

obedience. I still want to believe that God makes exceptions—even for me—but some of my proudest moments have come because I did not expect myself to be the exception to the rule. While I do believe we are loved even when we do not make the sacrifices we could make, I think part of this life is learning to love what we are capable of. I'm not often inclined toward obedience for the sake of obedience, but there are times, like the year I paid my tithing on our student budget with the money I'd earned selling my art, and I did it with tears of frustration in my eyes. I handed over an envelope to my bishop, and there was no miracle influx of cash that showed up later that month to reward us for our obedience. It even took me several months to feel okay about my decision to give the last of our money, but I am not worse for the experience. I never asked Vanessa and Gabriel why they did what they did or exactly what came because of it, but years after I was with them in Uruguay, they sent me a photograph of their family, the oldest daughter in her baptism dress, two more sisters born since we'd left, standing proudly in front of their older sisters. The new house in the background is still small, still poor. Gabriel likely works at the orange factory; Vanessa is prettier still. In the photograph, I can see they are beaming, proud of the life they have built for themselves.

ONCE, AS MY COMPANION and I walked home for lunch in the border town of northern Uruguay, we came down a street we did not know and found a large man stirring something in an even larger pot. Curious, we stopped to ask him what he was doing, and he explained that each day one person took the pot and cooked for all the families in the neighborhood. They pooled together what rations they received from the government and ate together every night.

From the hill, we walked to the church that stood near the edge and watched Magdalena's baptism. She crocheted for a living and only allowed us to come over when her husband was at work. And Paula, who had a hair studio in her home, wore bright red lipstick and sang so loudly, wearing her high heels and displaying her cleavage without noticing that no one else wore miniskirts to church.

I saw poverty in the city of Riviera that was beyond my scope of understanding. The smell of mildew and old cooking oil, the crisp color of mud floors and worn cardboard boxes and dirty barking dogs, the teen girls that came to the fence every morning asking to use my hair straightener before they went to school, the time a woman fed us moldy squashes for lunch and we all knew it and ate anyway.

I explained once to a concerned boy we were teaching that no, the body of Jesus would not in fact be under the white sheet that covered the sacrament table. In the church, the piano I played was so out of tune I often could not tell if the hymn I was playing was the song the congregation was singing.

Maybe the thing I remember best, though, is that distinct feeling I got every time we approached a new door or person on the street, the way, despite experiencing so little quantifiable missionary success to speak of, I felt sure that we were about to meet the golden contact, the one or ones I'd been sent on my mission to find, the person or family that had been praying us to them.

Some afternoons we worked on the rural outskirts of town and were often welcomed into houses by old and lonely people. With absolute impatience, we often found ourselves trapped in sparse living rooms or on the edges of rickety beds just listening while they, propped up by flat pillows, talked without any desire for another half to take part in the conversation. Honestly, hours I spent listening without getting a word in. I often could not follow their line of thought because it zigzagged so rapidly and nonsensically across the decades of their life. Spanish, still a new language, felt jumbled and clumsy because they almost never had a full set of teeth to work with.

We once left a home with a woman who spoke at us for hours without our even mentioning our purpose as missionaries. When we finally left, I, in frustration and anger, complained to my companion about what we were even doing out here in this uncared-for bit of desolation at the edge of a poor town listening to people talk nonsense for hours when we had the words that could save them.

"No," my companion, a native to the country, said, "We are not here to save them. We are only here to minister to them."

When I boarded a plane a year later to go home, I had not saved anyone. The thousands of lives I brushed up against left a mark on me, and I left a mark on some of them. My companion was right. We did not save. Through the grace of God we ministered with the kind of charity that grows between strangers, and more often than not, we were the ones ministered to.

Redemption

W HAT I WANT TO TELL YOU as you read these stories is that I've both found and lost God a hundred times over. In fact, maybe I've never actually found God at all, but imagining that I have indeed found something so much larger and more beautiful than I can explain is most often enough for me. I believe that somewhere in all this, we belong to parents who love us with that fierce and tender love reserved for the moments when you observe a child trying their best at something. I believe we have parents who are as proud of us as I felt of Remy and Thea when, despite the briskness of the afternoon, they tore off their clothes and went running across the sand and into the cold Northern California waves in pursuit of all the beauty and delight this world may have to offer. When I looked out over the ocean, the waves crashing against the faraway rocks, a pelican soaring wordlessly through the blue sky, I saw for a brief moment the incomprehensible largeness of the place with infinite beginnings and endings both behind me and in front of me.

I've both found and lost God a hundred times over—I sense a powerful, parental, guiding love from heaven. I think it feels like the joy I felt when I set down all I had been carrying and ran out to my children, letting the cold waves crash over us, holding their hands when the waves tugged at our feet, the sand crabs leaving bubbling holes as they dove into wet sand. My daughter lifted her feet and let the water pull her out while I lifted her. For me, Mormonism does not provide the ease of certain answers; it provides a language and the impetus to write about an afternoon on a beach and truly believe that maybe for that moment I had found God, or else something perhaps as holy—godliness.

A FEW WEEKS AFTER MY SIBLINGS and I were sealed to my parents in the Provo Temple, we hitched up a trailer and taped a sign on the back of our VW bus that said "Tehachapi or Bust." Mother Nature welcomed us in this unremarkable California town. My brother and I spent our days in her arms, climbing trees, collecting turkey feathers, building clay pots among the oak trees. It was in Tehachapi where the missionaries drove the canyon road and our long, steep driveway each week to teach me the lessons before I was baptized. Once they asked, "Does God love all people, or only good people?" Wanting so much to impress them, I spun around once in my chair and said, "Only the good people." "No," they said, "he loves all people just the same."

This last summer I visited Tehachapi again for the first time in twenty-five years. I was surprised to find that the dreamlike details that had so long visited me were precise memories that led me right back up the canyon and to the foot of my old house. The driveway gate was locked, so we drove the few acres around back on the chance that the old inhabited trailer that belonged to a neighbor was still there. A family came curious onto the rutted dirt drive. We asked if we could peek through their fence at my childhood home and property. "Of course," they said from the trailer that was still standing and housing people two decades later; it was dilapidated, with various shanty-like add-ons, while a small girl holding a scruffy stuffed rabbit stood between her pregnant mother and her father, who wore a baseball cap over his sandy hair.

The little girl approached my children as we walked across the uneven front yard made of dirt and roots, and soon the three of them were talking as if all children in the world were at some time, not so long ago, already friends. They were so kind, and my husband and I cried as we drove away about the sacredness of life even in the unseen and unsightly pockets of this world. Ten minutes before as I peered through the fence, I swear I saw the ghost of my seven-year-old self playing next to my round-faced brother, contemplating what it meant that God really loves all people just the same.

EVEN AS A KID, I was so intent on doing right, so devastated by doing wrong. Once, after talking at the back of the classroom with my friend in sixth grade, my teacher gave us the task of writing "I will not talk in class" one hundred times. I was so mortified at the thought of being in trouble, of having to face my parents and to live with such a mark on my history that I got to crying, and then could not stop. I cried through recess, through every single one of my hundred lines, and on to the parking lot where I cried and waited for the carpool.

My little son has inherited this propensity for feeling guilt at imperfection. The other day, after he had accidentally hurt the neighbor kid, I found him out the back door, facing the fence and staring into the overwhelming fog of a future of insufficiency. A few days before, he asked me in his most his earnest voice on our way home from the grocery store, "Mom, why did Jesus die for us?" I stumbled over the largeness of the question and wondered, at what point does one ever really grasp that another person died for them out of love and for a purpose infinitely larger than I can put words to?

But as I get older, I look back and see that in my moments of sadness, even at such a young age and sensing I was a

foreigner in a big world, I was held up by something more than reason, more than any explanation, more than knowledge, or more than even my parents. A spirit that is soft, unassuming, and patient held me, helped ease the pain of mistakes that surely would have led me to damn myself. So while I do not have the perfect words to say to my son, Christ did die for him as he did for me, and I have to trust that my son will be healed by that idea, as I am still learning to be.

DURING MY FIRST WEEK at the Missionary Training Center the teacher asked us to create a timeline listing prophets from Adam to the present day. I sat there in my long skirt, pen poised, and looked around the room at my missionary classmates scribbling away, only to realize that I had no idea what to write. I grew up in Provo, Utah; I went to seminary through high school; my parents had been baptized when I was young, but still, when it came to words like *apostasy*, I did not quite know the facts or timelines. I'd somehow missed these details.

Embarrassed at my own lack of knowledge, I wondered what I was doing embarking to another country to teach people this gospel when I clearly knew so little about these timelines, facts, lessons, and history. But I made it to Uruguay, and I sat in poorly painted kitchens at nights with old women and tried to teach them what I knew. I sat with families, a kid on either side of me, while we opened scriptures and read. I walked hundreds of miles on uneven roads in the pursuit of spreading the gospel, not because I could logically point to reasons, but because when I truly taught from my heart, the gospel seemed to turn a thousand colors of beautiful pastel that I wanted everyone to see.

It turns out, all these years later, I never really got good at tracking the details, but I did learn that something beyond timelines got me on a mission and keeps me returning to church each week in the decade since—the same spirit of comfort that upheld me as an awkward teen girl when I was nominated for prom queen but was not asked to go by anyone, the same spirit that reassured me of the possibilities of grandeur the morning I hiked through the mountains with my dad and an eagle flew overhead and sailed down the canyon in front of us. I believe in heavenly parents who love us in the way I love my children in my wholly unselfish moments.

Somehow, in all the small understanding I possess, there has been a greater spirit inhabiting my life. It is a spirit that tells me there is both unimaginable beauty and jagged shards of pain as we work out our own salvation. I know I am not special in feeling this. Our humanity intersects with a wide sky of ancient stars, and somehow, we belong to both spaces.

MY FRIEND ASKED ME IF I could write about something ugly because not all of what we encounter in a spiritual life is beautiful. My husband told me a story from his friend, a story about judgment, that still haunts me because I know there are times in my own life where I offer judgment instead of care, when I extend rigid instead of open arms.

There was a man who was baptized mere weeks before a big church conference in his stake. He came early from a relatively far distance the night of the big meeting to help usher the crowds. Upon his arrival one elder from the ward asked if the man had a suit jacket he was planning on wearing. When the man said no, the elder told him he needed to go home and get one before he came back. The man left but never returned.

I cringed the first time I heard it. Subsequent retellings do not make it better. But that story, along with the beautiful ones, is also mine to tell. I must confront that story if I am to be honest about my own shortsightedness.

Through human nature I falter with selfishness, judgment, and unkindness at times. I want to be healed, and so I

come to church to sing, pray, and listen with my community, and sometimes, in those rare moments when I am absolutely still to my own desires, I am healed, and sometimes I am not yet ready for healing. I do not know the ways or times in which the weaknesses of my heart will be made stronger, and so I go, every week, back to church, to prayer, to scriptures, to the most basic principles I was taught as a child. With bread and water I promise again that I will try to remember Christ, that I will try to make my actions exemplify his. Again and again I go back with the hope that I will become better.

I MADE A BANNER that said "Be Brave" out of some old fabric I had dyed. I sewed it to a ribbon, and as I walked my kids to preschool one afternoon, we stopped at a set of trees that I knew many college students from the campus we lived on would pass by and tied the banner in place. For my whole life, no matter how hard I've tried, my work cannot escape from looking handmade, and so as the letters swung in the breeze, the banner looked anything but crisp and professional. I suspected that the banner would be taken down by campus security, vandalized, or blown down by wind and rain, but every so often my Remy, Thea, and I would take that path to school to check on our words in the trees, and there they remained, brave and immutable fabric vigilantes.

About six months into the lifespan of the banner, the once colorful fabric had faded to white in the sun, and some of the letters fallen loose from the ribbon sagged as if their heads hung down. I meant to go back and tend to the letters, but I never went. I imagined that soon the sign would be pulled down and stuffed into a nearby trashcan. We went by a few weeks later though, and it still hung and looked better than before. Someone had tended to the drooping letters by hand-stitching them back onto the ribbon. A few weeks after that, we noticed that someone had placed bright, curly ribbons along the banner. Then a few weeks after that, we saw that someone had painted each letter with glow-in-the-dark paint so those two words, *Be Brave*, would shine in the darkness.

Nearly a year later I was giving a seminar to a group of students on campus when I mentioned the sign as part of a project that felt meaningful to me. I talked about how the sign had been adopted by the community and about the power of pursuing the projects we feel we should, even when we have no way of projecting what they might mean to us or to someone else. When I dyed the fabric a deep blue, traced and cut each letter and sewed them onto the ribbon, and set out to tie the words up somewhere, my kids pulled at my elbow and needed something from me every minute. I did not feel entirely brave, but I felt the desire to be, and the thing that never fails to surprise me is how the doing of something usually necessitates precisely the thing you were hoping to have.

At the end of the seminar, a boy who always sat in the back came to me and said, "You can never know what that banner meant to me. I never imagined I would meet the person who made it." He said that each morning he would ride his bike to school and see that banner waving him on. He said he felt like it had grown from the earth just for him. It came at a time when his heart hurt and he did not know how to heal it, but each day he was brave.

I cannot calculate the good I might do with these small acts, but I'm learning to trust in my intuition. That permutable place where so many of my thoughts, ideas, and actions seem to stem from show me again and again that there is spiritual power in using our creativity.

The more I experience the elegance of the unplanned, the intersection of people and ideas I could not have predicted, the more I believe God is a creative God and that we are imbued with the same spirit of creativity. I believe in a God who champions my imagination. I believe in that same God who will send a tender mercy to a boy whose heart was broken and needed to see the words *Be Brave* rising up from some unknowable source to send him on his way each morning.

TWELVE MORE TIMES I PRAYED

To SAY THANK YOU. When a woman at church stopped me and gave me an envelope with money for Christmas. After the park, in the car when my son told me it was so quiet near the trees, he stopped and prayed. When I saw my daughter for the first time and the doctor said, "She is a goddess, just like her name." On a plane home from Uruguay, I swear I saw an angel just beyond the wings as I looked out over the clouds. I prayed to say sorry. When I needed comfort. I prayed for my heart to be made soft and pliable. My students in a third-grade art class I teach, when for just a few minutes, every child stopped their fidgeting and listened to me as I talked about the importance of making self-portraits. When my load was too heavy to carry on my own. When my friend's brother committed suicide the night before my son's birthday, I prayed without words. Once I was careless and caused sorrow to my dearest friend on this earth. My prayers were thick with regret, and I promised never to be careless with someone I loved again. I prayed she would be taken care of in all the ways she needed. The weight of loss lifted like a rising balloon from my heart when we became friends again—the weight of the lifting of those years felt like a

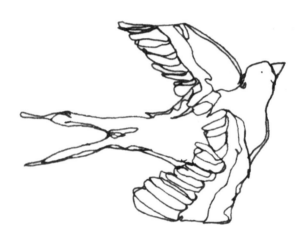

constant prayer that was answered in a hundred ways I could not have planned or predicted.

MY FATHER-IN-LAW is the kind of person who gladly took the job of hoisting a rotted-out hot tub from a vacant lot into the back of his old blue truck and back into his own driveway for about $30 pay. My husband, who somehow also got pulled into the Thanksgiving afternoon hot-tub job, says as they lifted the tub—the wet, heaving mass of soggy, rotten foam and wood—there was a moment when he thought he and the other two workers would drop it.

The men trying to hold up the tub with my husband, though employed by my father-in-law, were hardly employable. His workers are drug addicts with too much past to consider turning in a resumé somewhere, jail-goers, even a thief who once broke into his home and took his wife's jewelry. They are often sick, usually skinny as dried cornstalks, but they always give a firm handshake when they show up for holiday meals with our family. Usually when we visit, there is at least one of his employees staying in some corner of the house. One slept in a sleeping bag on the couch for months, long after he was able to do any work, while some sickness slowly took over his body. My father-in-law is their last chance for any sort of job or acknowledgment, and so they do what he asks without question.

On that afternoon though, under the hot tub, they were not enough, and they started to slip under the weight as they struggled to get the load into the truck. My father-in-law, in his uniform flannel, with fingers like sausages, stepped in and raised his thick arms and with a great burst of brute strength made the final hoist. My husband says he will never forget seeing his father's hands reach up, clutching the wood and filth, as his fingers sliced through an Oregonian yellow slug. His father did not even notice but wiped the slime onto his jeans and jumped into the driver's seat. I however, cannot forget last Christmas, when I looked out the kitchen window while I washed dishes and saw him sitting with my small daughter in a white plastic chair in the carport while she curiously touched his beard, and together they reached down to pet the old dog.

ONE HUMID SUMMER AFTERNOON, Remy got to missing his dad, who was in Japan doing fieldwork. After searching around the house, I found him in the backyard sitting on a rock and crying tears that were so sincere and alone that I immediately cried right along with him—out of both empathy and also a sense of joy that he, after a mere five years on this earth, was able to feel so deeply for someone else.

Because I was crying, I was short on words, but I carried him inside to an overstuffed chair and let his little heaving body fill in every space on my stomach and chest. We stayed there for a long time without speaking while he calmed—he seemed to want to melt right into me until any hurt he felt was gone.

I had already been thinking a lot about bodies and the spirit, but that moment brought new clarity to my abstract ideas and tentative conclusions. My body is home to my children. I lie between my children each night while they fall asleep, and they reach out in the dark and stroke my face or reach for my hand. It's like the reaffirmation of both their place in the world and their place in a larger plan, as they run their tiny hands across the familiar and tangible landscape of my body. My body for them is a manifestation of home, and home is what the spirit has always felt like for me.

There have been times in my life, more than I'd like to admit, that I've spent copious amounts of thought and energy trying to rearrange the home of my body. Roughly pushing furniture around with dissatisfaction, barging in with the latest trend, sitting at the window wishing my home was anything other than what it was. I think, like many, I've been harsh to my body, spoken unkindly to and about it.

In high school and college, I quickly learned that what my body looked like was actually important; my social survival felt like it depended on it in a culture where dating and marriage felt directly equated with self-worth. My body didn't always live up to my expectations though, or often to those of others, and I found myself fighting a banal war hoping for my body to be something other than what it was—read: *skinnier.*

Watching Thea move through the world with almost comical confidence has shifted my paradigm. Since she has been around, I slowly, one step and one day at a time, began reclaiming confidence in my body. I feel fierce in protecting her confidence, and I've learned in order to do that I have to protect my own. I've learned that in order to be an efficacious woman with any sort of spiritual power, I first have to love my body.

I want to love the place that is home to my spirit and home to my children. As I held my crying son, his head pressed up against the place where my heart beats, his legs wrapped around a belly I at one time despised for not being flatter, I felt a communion consecrated by the peace I've found with my body. I stopped worrying about remaking it into the perfect arrangement.

It is not just the maternal characteristics that make my body an important and vital spiritual vessel, though. The bodies of my friends who don't have children have been places of respite for my children and me, again and again. It is also not just the feminine that makes a body home. I still remember the feel of Carl's hand in mine when I was in labor—his touch kept me grounded to the earth, his body my peaceful home for that time. I watch my children run into the arms of my friends or nestle into their laps to read a book. They find serenity in the safe place of another's body.

As a kid and teenager, the phrase "the body is a temple" did not resonate with me because the real temples I knew felt so stark and ordered and white. When I stop and listen to my body, it is wild like a meadow or a secret mountain lake. It is not stark—it is not slight. It is full with the curves of my grandmothers and great-grandmothers. It is full with life and thousands of experiences worth remembering. For so long, it didn't quite fit the model I assumed it needed to in order to be beautiful or valuable. The idea of trying to make it a temple felt abstract, and it felt so far from where I was.

But now, a temple to me just means home. Temple means a place of rest from the world. Temple means fullness and complexity, a hope for better things along with acceptance, even if things do not get better than they are now. That day with my crying son, for the first time in maybe ever—

initially for my children and then for me—I recognized this body of mine as a temple.

As I was looking through an old journal, I came across a line I wrote for myself that simply said, "Think about the word *redemption*." I drove across town to deliver some freezer meals to a working single mother in my ward over the weekend. The thin driveway was cluttered with a limp bicycle wheel and a rusted car part, and as I stood at the front door I looked up to another apartment's sliding glass door, smudged with small-handed goop, damp from the inside morning heat against the cold air. No paint around the window frames was white, but I could tell it once had been. The woman opened the door to me. Her house smelled clean in the way that old apartments can never fully be clean, and her eighteen-year-old son who slept on a bed that encompassed the entire living room pulled a quilt up over his head. The scene was not beautiful to me. It was a type of hard that I have not touched and cannot pretend to really understand.

The gesture some other mothers and I made in putting together freezer meals for her felt almost laughable in light of hardship, but then I thought about that word *redemption*.

There are many difficult life circumstances—single motherhood among them—I cannot speak to for lack of personal experience. But maybe after all, if Mormonism has taught me nothing more than a dogged and indisputable desire to better understand these things, and to try to be a balm of Gilead wherever I go, my spiritual journey is not in vain. While I'm not exactly sure what redemption looks like, it seems I felt something of it in the hug the woman gave me as I stood in her front door, halfway between the wild world and the warmth of the home she had created with so little.

Strong

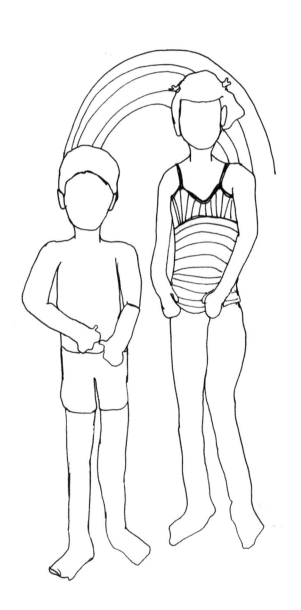

I CANNOT FORGET the afternoon my son ran down a rocky trail at a frantic pace, slipping on loose rocks and nearly skidding across his small, hardly firm knees, crying "I want to go home." I hurried behind, with helpless calls to calm him. I could not run fast because I carried Thea in a pack on my chest because she refused to walk anywhere, and how could I mind because she still laid her head against my heart while we hiked.

By the time I made it to the bottom of the trail, Remy was in the car seat, buckles strapped across his heaving and tiny chest. He had thick, wet streaks across his red cheeks. I told him to take some deep breaths, and I struggled to unhook the baby carrier across my back. Rain began to run at me as I ducked into the car. There was no lightning. There had been no lightning all day, and there were no signs of lightning in forecast. The rain was just a reprieve from the heat as gray crops of clouds turned quickly to rain that afternoon.

Remy's intense and almost abnormal fear of lightning came, I believe, from our summer in Sweden. We were at a beach one morning when a terrific storm blew across the water and over us in a matter of minutes. The thunder shook the trees, and we ran through the forest to the nearest bus stop. But the bus did not come for forty minutes, and Remy wailed under the feigned refuge of a tree branch the whole time we waited. A sincere fear overtook his three-year-old body, and he wept until that bus came. And even then, the bus driver was outraged that we needed to fit strollers onto the bus, and so there were Swedish curse words and a man who fought with the bus driver. And then we made it home, and I'd accidentally left the upstairs window open, and water flooded the spiral wooden staircase. And then I wept because I was so tired of making needless mistakes.

So I suppose Remy's fear of lightning is somewhat founded, but it is still surprising to see the fear drive him so powerfully. As we drove away from the trail that day, though, I thought of myself. I thought about how, although I do not literally run down trails screaming about what I believe will crush me, I often metaphorically do.

Over the last years I have done the work of unbinding my heart. Unraveling the threads that I thought it needed bound so tightly to stay good. I spent years in fear of where my heart might go if I untethered it. Fear that it would run from holiness and God and sacred things if I simply let it wander and explore. Fear that it might question itself beyond retention or lose its grip on awe.

Looking back, I can see myself running recklessly away

from what I thought would be my demise—a true walk into the unknown realms of my spirituality, away from pretense, away from rules and checklists and shoulds and shouldn'ts. Steps that I originally thought were headed away from a God and away from my spiritual self, but were in fact paths that unexpectedly led me nearer to him.

Not long after the rainy hike, I sat in the backseat of my sister's car during a 10:00 p.m. lightning storm. We were out by the lake, and the lightning glinted out from under the thick clouds. The clouds reminded me of a comfortable white dress a mother would wear, and the lightning, without order or apology, lit up the sturdy mountains that surround the valley like stalwart ancestors.

I wished Remy, asleep next to me, could have seen it. This is the beauty I wanted to explain on the drive home after he was so scared—that yes, lightning is to be feared at times, but he need not run from all things that offer the possibility of hardship. There is a time to run home, back to the familiar, back to the safety of all that is known, but there is also a time to untether your heart and let it go, even far, in search of the God you want to know.

When I listen to the steady and most familiar beat of my own heart closely, it does not misguide me. There is so much beauty in the God I thought I had understood, but I sense there is so much more. There is beauty in being surrounded by the darkness as I understand that what I really know is so small, a strike of light in an expansive sky, and still my effort is loved. The lightning that strikes far to the southwest lights up a mountain face you realize you have lived so close to all your life but have never gone to. Go there, is what I wanted to tell Remy, go there and come back often to tell me what you discover. I will be gathering what I can as well.

SEVENTEEN TIMES I FELT STRONG

THE DAY BEFORE I HAD REMY, I sat in a classroom listening to a reading by Terry Tempest Williams when I felt a single contraction so strong I thought the world had moved. I did not say a word but silently rejoiced at the power of my own body and the power of the boy who would be born the next day. Again I felt strong during labor with Thea. Each time a contraction came, Carl recounted a memory of ours in vivid detail, and several times, in the midst of the pain, I smiled as I thought of our life. As a young girl when I finished writing my first journal. When I stayed up all night painting in my studio in college. When I fasted a full twenty-four hours. When I thought about my baptism and what I promised to do because of it and tried in earnest to mourn with those that mourn and comfort those in need of

comfort. When after forty hours, my son came into this world with his eyes wide open. When my daughter knew instinctively how to get milk from my breast minutes after meeting me for the first time. When instead of saying a prayer in my bed I got down on tired knees and spent a long time with my forehead pressed to my clasped hands. When I was kind in disagreement. When I knew I could help to make change. When I knew I could ask people to listen to my voice. When I planned a service project for our ward Christmas party and all the children brought one of their own toys to wrap and give to a group of children in need. When I watched my husband sitting cross-legged with the children in his nursery class. When my children invited an outsider to play. When I read the stories of my ancestors. When I tell my own story.

THINGS I CAN STOP BELIEVING

THAT IF I GOT in a car crash, the parts of my body covered by temple garments would not be harmed. That my children will misbehave if I miss days of reading the Book of Mormon. A Young Women medallion is the ultimate indicator of my teenage dedication to the gospel. That I will have to make up for not earning my medallion by completing the program if I am ever called to be a Young Women leader. That it is wrong or weak to cry when giving a talk or speaking about spiritual things. That if someone does not cry at spiritual things, their feelings or experience are less real. That it is hard to know more about Heavenly Mother. That I must simply be lacking faith if I do not agree with something I am taught in a church meeting. That God is eager to find fault.

A FEW SUMMERS AGO, Carl, Remy, Thea, and I drove through the Norway mountains for three days, winding our way to a final camp in a town called Selje that felt so far away from anything I have ever known it may as well have been a dream. Carl was there on a geologic pilgrimage to see a rare set of rocks called eclogites—rocks that were once carried one hundred miles down into the earth and then brought back to the surface over hundreds of thousands of years through tectonic shifts, molten channels of earth, and a lot of luck. As for me, I was unsure about what type of pilgrimage I was on.

At dawn we drove on high planes beyond the fjords. The lighting was hazy and pink as if the sun knew it lacked proper rest, and I felt much the same way. I looked up and out the window just in time to see two moose with heads bent to the ground, the morning fog tucked softly around them. Their largeness, otherworldliness, and serenity shocked me. The image passed too quickly to even form words to tell my husband. I saw in them something I wanted for myself—graceful confidence at their place in the world, beloved creatures not at odds with God, but cared for deeply. I envied their simplicity. I wanted to stand in my own place with that peaceful assurance, but in the midst of so much beauty I was experiencing extreme spiritual unrest. I tried to put the lid back on my heart to keep it from overflowing.

In Selje, we were alone on the beach. My children played in the pearl-colored sand, the warm turquoise water lying still and clear as glass. A solitary fish brushed past my calf as I stood a distance out and looked back at a white wooden church perched eloquently and unused at the edge of the beach.

At noon I got into the car to head back to our campsite to grab lunch. I stepped on the gas pedal, and with grand and jarring interruption, I backed directly into a boulder jutting up out of the middle of the road. With the bumper of our rental dented and my hungry children waiting, I put my head in my hands and cried a hard and bitter cry. It was a culminating cry, drawn out of me by our drive through this foreign land of Norway. I was ripe with every doubt and difficulty I'd ever had with religion. In the place where absolute surety and comfort once lived, now confusion, bitterness, and sadness surfaced from the depths of my spirit.

I was there in the middle of a dreamlike world that felt serene and placid, the colors more vibrant than anything I had ever experienced, yet my heart and mind were not at peace. The deeper we drove, the more constrained I felt by the faith of my upbringing, as though the majesty of the place was bursting through the seams of the world as I had known it. Surreal bodies of water, the moose, majestic fjord cliffs, a dozen teenage boys jumping off a dock into deep, clear water at the bottom of a steep flourishing valley as the sun lolled low in the sky. It was all too much and too beautiful, all that grandeur looming in juxtaposition with what I thought I had to say I knew for sure. I could not bear the idea that I possessed a fullness of truth that none of these people would likely ever have access to, or even care to. The weight of having to believe every thread of my Mormonism felt too heavy to bear.

I felt rough and lazy in my knowledge of the sublime and presumptuous in believing I comprehensively understood much of anything in this world, let alone about the ones before and after this life. Backing into the rock with the rental car, the crunch of metal on stone, outwardly manifested the panic and claustrophobia I felt on the inside. This was the pinnacle of my crisis of faith.

I finished crying in the car and drove back to the campsite. I knew I could not remain in such a place of pain as I sorted out my place in Mormonism. I sensed that while God intends for us to be fully ensconced in life's challenges, such a perpetual state of perceived crisis could not be a method of progression sustained by the God I had come to know. At the campsite, in the tent by myself, I knelt on a sleeping bag and said a prayer with no words. My heart was broken, and my spirit was contrite. When I stood again minutes later, I understood one thing—I could no longer give my spiritual questions and wanderings the name of "crisis." I could not continue pelting my own sincere heart with stones of shame and guilt because I did not believe perfectly, or understand perfectly, or even sustain a constant desire to do either of those things.

I drove back to the beach, and my children were still there, so content and simple, with Carl. Such grand little creatures— it was as if they were held in the palm of God, right there on that beach in a place so far from home. We hiked along the shore together until we came to the place where the eclogites were. I do not know what I was expecting, but I would never have known by looking at them that these rocks had been one hundred miles under the surface of the earth and were then driven by extreme pressure—reformed and metamorphosed, their elements changed completely over millions of years by both heat and cold—until they showed up like they always

belonged on this peaceful shoreline. They were the color of Christmas trees and rubies. Small patches on the rocks, some in the form of small garnets, glittered in the sunshine. Carl ran his fingers over them, and I knew for him they were holy reminders of both how brief and how sacred our lives are.

The next day we arose early and drove away from that campsite, past the beach and eclogites we will probably never return to. I did not leave with answers to all my questions, but I did leave the word *crisis* behind, buried in white sand in front of that quiet church.

Since then, my eclogite-like crisis has moved deeper and deeper into the molten, mysterious mantle of my heart. It has been heated to extraordinary temperatures, changing its properties and molding into something entirely different. I am not sure exactly when or how it will resurface, but I eagerly wait for that moment, perhaps far off, when I will see it in some other dreamlike landscape. I will run my fingers over it in amazement because it will sparkle in a way I could not have predicted, in a way it did not before. It will no longer be my crisis, but rather my story molded by a thousand broken hearts and contrite spirits, metamorphosed by a thousand more moments of sublime and inexplicable hope and joy. Not a crisis now—just my story, the surprising story that was one of faith all along.

Tradition

M Y MORMONISM started long before me, with a grandmother of five greats. She was supposed to marry a Danish boy in a small town south of Copenhagen, but instead, she got on a boat and sailed west. I heard the full story from my aunt who is the keeper of our family history, and I performed it to a ukulele tune with my husband at a Primary Pioneer Day activity. We treated the tale like a polished, everyday object—my great, great, great, great, great-grandmother's faith that something would be waiting for her when she arrived in Zion. Stories like this often steady my small boat in the rolling and sometimes unpredictable waves of spirituality. Something in the stories that came before keeps me afloat, eyes to the horizon line, destined for some Zion I cannot fully comprehend.

Carl and I were married in Manti, Utah, because I felt the inexplicable calling to do something sacred in the land my ancestors settled when they had finally arrived at the place they left Denmark for. I think back on that day often, the way Carl and I walked out of the temple doors beaming like two tulips in bloom, and I looked out over the green September valley. I felt surrounded by celebrations both of the people I could see in front of me and of the ancestors that had lived there long ago.

Some days I am the strongest skeptic of my own internal faith, a disbeliever in my own belief, but some days I am filled with a hope that the past and the future do matter greatly, that the people who fill both of them are somehow connected to me, that there is before and after, eternal rounds, people linked to each other by forces so powerful that they might visit me on our wedding day, when my children are born, and when I die, passing through a veil back into their open arms.

THINGS I CAN BELIEVE BETTER

THAT MY STORY IS WORTH TELLING. That my story does not need to please all people. That belief is a choice made again and again. Belief can exist in spite of frustration. Belief and its opposite can arise unbidden. That the church can be a better place for my daughter, as well as my son. That my daughter will get to go on as many church camping trips and long hikes as my son will. That I will hear the voices and know the names of more female church leaders. That my prayers are answered through the actions of other people.

That I can be the answer to another person's prayer by my action. That my contribution in this world can extend beyond the children I raise. I do not have to excel at the domestic. I can better believe in the unique and quiet depth of spirit I feel during my hours as a stay-at-home mom. I can better believe in the choices I make based on the intuition I feel guiding me.

MORMONISM is the house whose halls I know best. It is the story I am not abandoning because it is the story I choose—and in many ways has chosen me—again and again to grapple with. Mormonism is my native spiritual language and many of the threads with which my life's tapestry is woven.

Picture a small cabin on a muggy, green field up against a deep wall of trees. Once as a teenager I visited the home that belonged to Joseph Smith's family. Together with my Catholic aunt, my mom and I were visiting her brother and his partner in upstate New York for our first mother-daughter vacation. On the first day, we drove a rental car toward Palmyra, New York. I sat between my mom, who in many ways was still a new Mormon, and my aunt, who was still slightly baffled by the way my mom no longer sipped wine with her at dinner, while my uncles unfolded maps and navigated the highways. I tried to be nonchalant about the adolescent anticipation I felt in making this pilgrimage toward the birthplace of the Book of Mormon and the first vision of Joseph that I'd imagined so much about.

The Smith cabin, at the end of a lonely dirt road in a flat meadow backed by a tall forest, felt both familiar and ordinary as the senior missionary guide talked about how the Smith children gathered nightly with their parents, about how Joseph learned in this very place to ask questions with the faith that they might be answered. I ran my hand over the table where they must have sat and recommitted myself to gathering my own family each night in a similar way. I pictured Lucy Mack Smith, and though I know little about her personally, a home breathes of the mother who lived there, even after a hundred years. We each dutifully examined the worn wood of the doorframes and nodded politely at the senior missionary as she explained each detail. The story of Joseph Smith had been inextricably bound to my own each year I'd grown older. In Primary we learned that he talked with God and Jesus in a forest, and as a small kid, I did not doubt for a moment that Joseph did see exactly what he said he did. As I got older, he turned nearly to a mythical hero who must have been a handsome and brave teenager when he walked into the Sacred Grove with the intent to pray,

before understanding the part he would play in changing the course of so many lives.

In the very spot where Mormonism was born, I was giddy with belief. We walked outside and followed signs to the Sacred Grove, my patient aunt and uncle giving me time and space to seek whatever significance I might be searching for out there. As I wandered, I kept asking myself, "Was it next to this tree?" "In this clearing?" "Around this bend?" I hoped that I might re-create something of the vision I'd grown up hearing about. I honestly thought maybe since I had been faithful enough as a kid, I could slip away from the others to receive my own personal encounter with God. I peered up into trees and tried to feel my way to the holy ground where Joseph prayed for a good hour, but before I saw any pillars of light, my aunt said something about being lost in this never-ending grove, and everyone chuckled.

I left those trees sans vision, sans any major spiritual movement within my heart, sans any prompting as to where the actual prayer of Joseph Smith even took place. But I did not leave with nothing. I carried a piece of hope from that plain, summer, sparkling forest. I carried the peace of a regular home where Joseph lived.

I recognized that my relatives—my mother's own brother and sister—did not understand what could be so important to me in that forest. But instead of demeaning my belief, they accompanied me there with a kindness that has only grown deeper and stronger in my family. I know this story I choose to unfold piece by piece is deeply complicated. I know now that the story of Joseph Smith is not as simple as my teenage self wanted and believed. For a time, that realization threatened to pull down the walls of the faith I grew up within. But it was not the walls being removed after all, but rather the scaffolding around a structure built to last.

Mormonism is the house whose halls I know best. I continue to walk them—with my toddler who cannot sit still in sacrament meeting, with the nursery children I teach, with the friend whose husband no longer accompanies her to church—into rooms of Mormon history I never knew existed, through entire wings filled with questions I've learned to be comfortable spending time with.

I think of my teenage self, walking through the sacred grove so many years ago, and I do not pity her for her naïveté. I do not feel sorry that she truly believed she might witness something miraculous. I am grateful that, even then, she was building a house before she knew what more it could become. In fact, when I look back now, I can see a light shining down on her as she wanders through that grove. She could not see it then, but even still, it lights the house she lives in with a welcoming and comforting glow that feels like home.

I F YOU DUG through my boxes of childhood, you may find tucked between the pages a photograph from my fourteenth year. Every element of the photograph would sing awkwardly with the familiar nostalgia of Mormonism. I am standing on the set of stairs that lead to the stage just outside the doors of the gym, the cinderblock painted a thick, glossy white. I am in a wedding dress, and I am clearly not amused. The wedding dress belonged to one of my Young Women leaders, who even at the time was smaller than I, and so the dress is not zipped in the back. Even at the time I felt it was ridiculous. The photograph now confirms that yes, my unibrow and untamed hair complimenting a poofy nineties wedding dress were completely ridiculous. I thought surely the young men in the ward were going to come bursting through the doors of the church at any moment, and there I would be, in all my unzipped fluorescent-lit glory.

But just the other day as Carl and I sorted out a box of his high school things, another picture fell from the pages of a notebook. It is Carl, skinny as ever and fifteen years old. He is dressed in attempted Book of Mormon warrior fashion— an oversized metal helmet threatening to bring him to the ground, a breastplate, a shield like a car door, and of course, the long and jewel-handled sword. Around the edges of the photograph is written, "Put on the whole armor of God."

I do not resent the contours of my Mormon youth experience. It simply is what it is. Carl and I can laugh ourselves silly looking at old photographs as we stoop over cardboard boxes of memories together in the hallway of our little house. However, I spent many subsequent years convincing myself that I was enough, even in my big-boned body, even when I did not go on lots of dates like so many of my college roommates, even when I was a returned missionary for several years and not married. And so, if I am ever a Young Women leader, you can be sure that those beaming little girls will not be convinced by me to pose in wedding dresses not their own. I believe the future of this faith is made up not only of white wedding dresses but of girls and women standing more confidently and resolute in whatever they choose to do. Let me be a part of leading them there.

CARL AND I sat with Remy and Thea on the floor of our living room. We were surprised to know that Remy was a step ahead of us when we pulled out the red leather scripture case that Carl used on his mission. "Those are scriptures," he said. "Jesus wrote them."

I am always surprised at the starring role Jesus plays in my children's lives. He is often an unfailing answer, an inconceivable comfort, a joy as exuberant and natural as a full moon rising over a mountain. I suppose that is the beauty of religion—the ideas and beliefs give us hope where none would be offered by logic. And then, because we are taught to nurture believing hearts, our shred of hope fuels action, which turns to a life in which we sit on the living room floor with our children on a Monday night.

Carl is in the final years of a PhD in geology at Stanford. Logic and long-range complex thinking is what he does for a living. But yet, there he is each week, helping Thea and Remy memorize, line by line:

Ask and it shall be given, seek and you shall find, knock and it shall be opened unto you.

As I have loved you, love one another.

My brilliant husband is an academic not immune to serious questions about the feasibility of almost any religious premise—and still, line by line, between children and father, they speak the metaphors, ask to be given unto, seek to find, knock to open, and repeat the principle to love. For us, whatever else is or is not true, there is value in this tradition for us, of willing our hopes, together, on the chance that someday it all really is just as glorious as we imagine.

Creativity

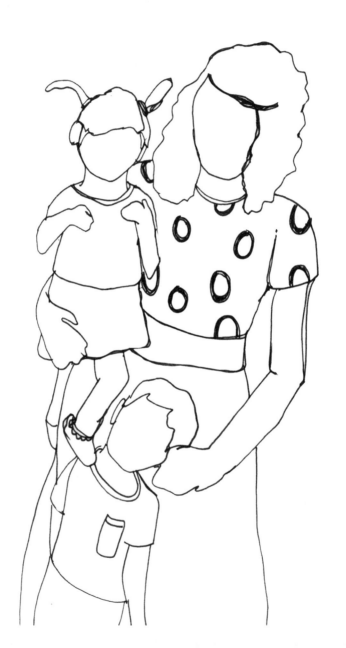

As a college student I was a collector of things that I sensed were valuable, things that told me a little more about the history I came from. So every time I visited the campus library, I gathered a few of the old cataloging cards spread out on the desks, repurposed as scratch paper. I loved the look of each typewritten word giving factual descriptions of forgotten books—tangible relics of a vast history I sensed I was part of. I was interested in what their clues might teach me, but I also wanted to give them new life, to repurpose them into something even more personal.

After collecting enough cards to fill a large backpack, I took them home and, with my rough sewing skills, stitched two together at a time, making square pockets of paper that could fit in the palm of my hand. I filled each packet full of wildflower seeds—I can still hear the sound of all those slight commas of seeds falling into paper. It felt as if they were ready for wherever I might send them. I sewed the open edge of each pocket shut and gathered them all in a basket. I took the seed packets to an unused vacant wall in a neighborhood in my city where I knew lots of people would walk by. Drab and painted several shades of nothing, the wall was perfect.

It was a Friday afternoon. It was a little cold, and I rubbed my hands, feeling both subversive and excited as I began taping a layer of plain pieces of paper in the shape of letters, spelling the word *grow*. On top of those I taped individual packets of seeds that people could take with them, leaving behind the plain paper spelling *grow*. When cars drove by, I acted as if I was doing something official, saying "hello" to curious onlookers as they walked past. The work took longer than I anticipated, and by dusk a friend showed up to help. It was dark, and we were working by streetlight when the neighbors from the house on one side of the wall came out to ask what we were doing.

As we spoke with them, the neighbors from the house on the opposite side of the wall joined us. The slight absurdity and ease of the project at hand made for natural conversation. As everyone taped card catalog seed packets to the half-done letters, the word *grow* slowly took shape. I smiled when one neighbor said to the other, "We've lived so close to each other for so long, but I've never met you. What's your name?"

As we put the last pieces onto the wall, a police officer arrived on the scene, lights ablaze and sirens wailing. He was perplexed at this crowd who apparently gathered to put a positive four-letter word on a wall in the middle of the city. Lacking grounds for getting us in trouble, he left.

After the last seed packet was in place, I posted instructions: "Please take a packet of wildflower seeds and write on the paper beneath it what you plan to do with them." Despite all the hard work, I was skeptical that people would participate but hoped for ingenuous responses. I walked back home, empty basket in hand, not bothered by the cold, a little reluctant to leave the project all alone. There was no assurance of success, but my happiness was not fazed. I had done something that felt important to me, and I had made new friends doing it.

Looking back at the wall from a distance I noticed the letters were a little off kilter—an exaggerated *W* dominated things. I saw something basic that strangers had built together in the hopes that it might mean something more.

When I returned the next evening, every packet of seeds was gone. In their place the wall still said *grow*, this time in the handwriting of so many different people. Much to my surprise, everyone who removed a packet took the project seriously.

I will bring the seeds to plant at my grandma's house that weekend

I'll take them with me on my business trip

These will go in a neighbor's yard

Plant them in my new garden

Take them up into the mountains

To the duck pond
To the tree where I used to nap at the park

On and on. I stood at the wall feeling overwhelmed by the web of complex humanity constantly being spun around me. I marveled to be part of such a nexus. I touched the papers, trying to imagine the person who had stopped to write there. I pictured them walking away, packet of potential wildflowers in hand.

This world has surprised me since I can remember. Somewhere there is an unexpected patch of wildflowers growing in an abandoned and colorless lot, bright and vibrant colors thriving where at some time, somewhere, their seeds were cast by some hopeful hand.

W HEN I WAS twenty years old I moved to El Salvador—not as a Mormon missionary, but as an eager college sophomore. Each night at five the rains came and pounded on our tin roof while we stayed in the ark of our little home. The country was as foreign as waking up in a new land after forty days of storm. The rain did not deter the wildness of the city. Buses barreled through puddles while men whistled—fingers to lips—when they wanted to get off, women stood under scant roofs and patted pupusa dough with their palms, children waited out under a bushy tree with their soccer balls, and then, as suddenly as the rain began, it stopped, and the whole world started up again, this time in wet and bright color.

For a summer I rode the bus each morning to a school in the middle of San Salvador. A school for boys with no parents—the most unruly and gentle bunch I had ever encountered. I was the art teacher, but mostly a student to their resourcefulness. We painted the walls of the dormitories with great long rollers taped to brooms. We drew and discussed, and I stumbled around with my college Spanish and high school soccer skills. I felt part of them. I felt at home. There is something that happens to the lonely and forgotten; there is room in the heart for anyone, and at that time, we were both lonely and a little forgotten. There was one boy in particular, Dario, who parted his night-black hair evenly every morning and had the skin of a porcelain doll, his face a rounded little seed. He excelled at everything we worked on. He rinsed the paintbrushes after class and cried the hardest when we left the school to go back home at the end of the summer.

Five years later I returned to El Salvador to stay with a friend, this time speaking fluent Spanish. One afternoon on the bus I looked across the aisle and recognized two boys from the school. I was doubtful they would remember me, but they spent some time staring at me and then called my name. Sweet, hardly grown boys navigating this wild world. I asked about Dario, and they said he had gone to school, a college nearby. He was taken care of in some way.

To me, the appearance of the boys on that bus felt like the return of the dove Noah sent out into the abyss. There are times when we send our hopes, fears, desires, questions out into the sky wondering if they will return with an answer, some evidence that God is listening at some reachable shore.

All the time we are deliverers of olive branches to one another. Our crossings are the miracles. Our offering sent out into the sky coming back with a note tied to the wing saying, "This universe is inexplicable. Let the miracles of your crossings be enough evidence to bring you back to shore safely."

WHEN I WAS PREGNANT with Thea, I sensed she was nervous to come here, so I spent nine months silently reassuring the rotating little planet in my belly that I would take good care of her. Several weeks after she was born, I made a bold decision to stay home from church, bold only in that I refused to give in to expectations I was overeager to hold myself to.

Thea and I stayed home while Carl and Remy went to church, and the memory of those three hours is my saving

grace at times. Nothing happened. We just stayed in bed, and I looked at her, buttery spring light coming through the window and onto my bed.

We are everyday making our own cathedrals; we are everyday renewing vows we once made to love as well as we can. We are born with the ability to worship—not laws, not perfection, not order, but God, and we do so in that inexplicable space where holding my daughter's hand felt as ancient and familiar as it did new. Memories like this mercifully give me pause from the noise of life. Expectations are a raucous bunch that would rather have you running around not feeling good enough than spending a moment in peace knowing you are.

ONE AFTERNOON while I sat upstairs on my bed and wrote then erased sentence after sentence, I listened to my Remy and Thea downstairs. They had set up elaborate formations of toys on either side of the room, and their game consisted of pushing every possible boundary in an imaginary world. They were excelling at play, and the world they ask me to enter with them again and again is that of play—a place without wrong answers, at least without the sort of questions that end the game. They work as small scientists, testing every hypothesis because they do not have the stultifying expectation for limits. They are not interested in what has been done or read or studied. My children pull me along into their world where play is mandatory because my world of answers bores them.

As an adult I've often interpreted Christ's instruction to become like a child as a call to meekness, humility, submissiveness. But this childhood world where I see my own children thrive is colorful, textured, a little unruly, unpredictable. It is not made of humility alone, or rather, it is made of the kind of humility required of true experimentation.

My children have taught me to play again. To become as a child is to believe in me as their mother. They play by moving their thoughts around, rearranging the world one hundred times in a day; they play by asking questions without guilt or embarrassment. They are unreasonable in their taking but also flawless in their giving. In a child's world, a paper heart actually does fix sadness, and when I am like a child, willing to extend grace to that offering, my sadness is lifted.

Play for my children consists of hours submerged in countless possibilities. Could we not do the same with our own spiritual lives? My children argue without guile and defend without one hundred percent certainty that they are right, just to see what defending the idea feels like. Could we not do the same with our faith?

The place where my children live is messy with experi-

ments, cluttered with piles they will come back to, and rooted in the safe harbor of home. At night my children pray by naming all the things they love. One night my son mentioned the birds at the ocean—how much he loves them, and I realized I had not thought lovingly about birds at the ocean in years. My son's four-year-old friend said the sun was a star, to which my son responded, "No, the sun is Jesus—right, Mom?" It took me a while to realize that he was too young to distinguish between a *u* and an *o*, and so to him, Jesus would be the sun. In the interest of not fostering confusion, I corrected the misunderstanding, but I will encourage his willingness to play with words, belief, and ideas.

I have discovered holiness in the exercise of abandoning my own world to enter the sacred lands of my children. Their birth—both my son and daughter and the personally uncharted territory one enters for months after a child is born—was all play, because schedules, reasonableness, and productivity were not at the forefront. We were at the beginning of writing a new story.

I believe we can find God in many ways. I believe our heavenly parents seek us out wherever we live, whether that be strictly in the mind, in despair and joy, in an office, or in nature. It is sometimes hard to recognize them or their efforts because we have already written their parts, made up our minds about what a spiritual life looks like. I know for sure, though, that when I stop and enter that space where my children are most comfortable—a space of play, imagination, and possibility—calmness enters in as I believe again that many things are possible.

A T THE BEGINNING OF SPRING I took my children on a walk at dusk, Remy riding his bike without training wheels for the first time as he gave himself over to the vulnerability of a moment when balance is not a guarantee. Over and over again I watched his little blue rain boot kick the ground and pedal like mad until he was headed somewhere. And then, as quickly as he was confident in his stride, he would stop, drop his bike, and run to a plant or bush near the path. He plucked leaves, berries, fronds, and seeds and stuffed them into his pocket until, satisfied, he told me, "I sure have a collection!"

In my own spiritual life, I have come to recognize that interval between the balance of surety and a continual stopping to touch the soft green hair of a rabbit's ear leaf, a fallen acorn, a delicate fern—seeing life anew again and again. I think of the New Testament story of the woman with an issue of blood—specifically of her hand reaching out into the clutter and chaos of a crowd, not sure that she would reach Christ, but nevertheless reaching for him in hope. Her story is sacred to me because she truly believed that by reaching outside of the bounds that her culture had set for her—perhaps even the bounds she had set for herself—she could be made whole.

Somehow, being witness to Remy's dogged reaching into each bush, tree, and hole in the ground with the belief that he would find something of value brought my own spiritual wandering into greater focus. My explorations are driven by a belief that in reaching outside of what I think I am capable of, I might touch the hem of a robe. I might be that unexpected person healed in the midst of a crowd. By reaching, I might be made more whole.

I HAD BEEN a full-time Latter-day Saint missionary for about a year when I was sent to a city that did not like missionaries, full time or otherwise. I'm not sure if reputations of previous missionaries tarnished ours, or if the dislike was due to the city's fervent dedication to a famous preacher who claimed he could offer plots of land in heaven in exchange for a microwave or a few hundred pesos. Maybe they were nervous to make any religious commitment that required much more than understanding they were saved. Whatever it was, the people in the town of Rivera crossed the street long before we had a chance to talk with them, and many of our days were spent clapping outside of gates while the people inside pretended not to hear us. The days were long and unproductive, and I had no choice but to feel that I was wasting my time in this hot city where the people we wanted to teach were making great efforts to avoid us.

One day we passed the city council building downtown. We had crossed through the park in front of the building every day. Sitting on the benches outside, trying to talk to people taking their lunch break, I had an idea that began to play itself out in my mind. I imagined what it would look like to have an art show in that building. The foyer was empty and large. The high ceilings and big windows cast a perfect light, and I saw people go in and out of the building all day.

I spent a couple of days talking my companion into believing that proposing an art show as a missionary was a good idea. I loved this companion dearly. She did funny things like turn a fan on full force while we slept, no matter how cold I was. She found mysterious ailments and pains that caused her to leave the house slowly after our lunch break. Our conversations often led to how she had never kissed a boy but very much wanted to. Still, I would not have found the courage to make the vision of a community art show a reality without her support.

With nerve bred of bravery, desperation, and faith and a

brazenness that comes with wearing a missionary name tag, we headed straight into the mayor's office, where we asked if we could have an art show in the grand foyer of the city's nicest building. We would donate the proceeds from any purchased art to buy winter coats for teens in an orphanage where we spent our designated nonproselyting service hours. To my surprise, the mayor, sitting behind a plain desk said, "Sure, we'd love to have you do that."

My companion was a good sport as we made plans during spare minutes in our apartment during lunch hour. The art show would be a series of two dozen black-and-white, large-scale photographs of people I'd met in Uruguay and had photographed in my time there. Through weekly emails and a mother who has always been willing to back my wild ideas, the photographs were printed in large format and shipped to me.

The week before the show found me on two local radio shows. I did the interviews from our tiny missionary desk in our apartment, fumbling around with my imperfect Spanish, hoping to convey some part of the love that I felt for the people I was trying to serve.

The night of the show, missionary elders from the nearby areas stood on the steps of the foyer and sang hymns as the people started to come in. I wore my best dress, thin and a little ragged from a year of constant wear.

The photographs of the people I had loved so much

throughout my year as a missionary hung all around me. Their eyes, complicated and with so many stories to tell, watched me and my companion as we greeted people.

Our appearance on the local news that evening did not mean fame for the church, but still, there we were, a pair of missionaries with a choir of young missionaries singing in the background on the news.

The mayor, a kind woman with tall hair and a fur coat for the occasion, introduced the show to the crowd that had gathered and gave us a warm hug as she introduced my companion and me. Many of the people who came were members from our ward, and they were so proud, both of me and of the church they belonged to. Many strangers wove in through the foyer as the night went on, and I talked with a few of them while the elders sang in the background.

One woman from our ward, a mom of young children, showed up later in the evening. As we stood in the middle of the foyer—people moving in and out looking at the photographs as they stared back at us—she put her arm around me and said, "We will never forget you here." It was such a kind thing to say, even when it could not have been entirely true. I'm sure they have forgotten me—the town, the members, the kids from the orphanage—or at least the details of me. What I imagine they might remember is that something out of the ordinary happened while we all gathered together that night. Somewhere there is a choir singing in the background of that memory, echoing a reminder that the spirit is not made of articulation and rules, but of risk. Taking a risk in that city of Rivera showed me I am capable of participating in unexpected moments of divinity right here on this earth, but I must be brave and trusting and risk an unknowable outcome in order to take part.

IN THE BEGINNING of Mark's Gospel, a paralytic man is lowered into a home by four of his friends who had broken a hole into the roof above the crowd. They know Jesus is teaching there, and the crowd was too pressing to enter in by the door. Hoping that Jesus will heal this friend, they climb up above and do something that I imagine was most unexpected and unconventional. I have read or heard that story so many times in my life, but it was not until recently, when I stopped to really consider the scene, that I was taken aback.

When I think of these people climbing on top of the roof while carrying their friend on his sickbed, about to dig a hole and interrupt a large crowd—not to mention the most important and sought-after man in the city—I wonder if they hesitated. I wonder if they thought they should turn back, that it was just a silly idea. But then, I marvel at their bravery—

breaking a hole in that roof and sending their friend right down where he landed at Jesus's feet. His reaction to this act now stuns me. He does not question—he does not lecture the people, saying they should have waited just outside the door. He simply accepts their offering of faith without question. He heals the man, first from his sins and then from his physical ailments—the man rises, picks up his bed, stands.

There I am in the group on the roof. I see myself hoping to come to the feet of Christ and sometimes doing it in ways that are not prescribed or by the book. Or there again, I am among the people pressed into that home to hear Christ. I wonder so much about those people. How did they react when the man was lowered? Were they upset at the interruption? Did they feel like the paralytic man did not deserve to come right to the feet of Jesus when they had waited a long time and endured the cramped surroundings to see him, to hear him? How do I think of people who are coming to Christ in ways that differ from my own? How do I treat them?

It is possible those people were harsh, but also—and I hope more likely—the crowd was nothing but kind and patient. What if everyone in that small room, gathered around Christ as he taught and healed the man, what if they celebrated in unison at the miracle they were a part of? What if their spirit contributed to the miracle? What if they marveled at the diverse paths that lead each person to Christ? What if they made

that room—ceiling hole and all—a holy place of acceptance and kindness and celebration where one of their brothers was healed, where because he was, they too might be?

Those friends on the roof mean so much to me. I see them there with quite the story to tell, and Christ does not for even a moment distrust their intuition or intention. In fact, he loves them dearly, does exactly the thing they want most—he heals them; he blesses them. I have felt this same love and acceptance from God in very quiet and personal ways—in prayer, in song, through my children, on walks outside, teaching nursery children, in hoping, praying, working for change, in valuing tradition.

Valuing tradition. Those people already gathered in the room—I think of how their stories deserve the same respect and kindness, even if they would never consider climbing on the roof. Something real and valuable brought them to that house too, brought them to the feet of Jesus. That front door is as familiar to me as that hole in the roof. Whether on the roof or in the room below, it is Christlike to assume that people are trying to do the best they can. I know I am a better person when I cultivate empathy, and I have been blessed for having received it from others. As members of the body of Christ, we are each responsible for creating a space not only of acceptance, but of joy and encouragement for our sisters and brothers and the stories they are working so hard to live well.

Zion

THINGS I WILL REVERENCE

MY SON WITH CLOSED EYES, folded arms, and a face toward the sky telling Heavenly Father thank you for the birds and the whales. The way he promises he will help people the way Jesus does.

The largest moon I ever saw. On the outskirts of a poor city in Uruguay with a newly baptized family full of children. I went home that night and painted the moon in my journal, and it covered up all the words I had written. It was so big, larger than my understanding and merciful in such a way that I truly felt I might reach out and touch it, grab hold of all the miracles in this world, and somehow keep them safe.

My grandparents, who died ten days apart. My grandpa went first, even though my grandma's body was filled with the final stages of cancer. He was hardly even sick. For ten days my grandma braved this world without him, then headed beyond as well, completing her two wishes—that my grandpa would not be left alone without her on this earth and that they would not be apart for too long.

The bird that flew through my open door and into my living room—that bird's momentary confusion until he found the way out the door and left my two children with the stark impression that anything is possible.

My daughter Thea, whose name derives from the idea that there is female deity. Before she was born, I sensed she was nervous to come. I reverence that still she chose me to care for her.

Long grass and red poppies bathing in morning sun earlier than they need to be up while they wait for someone to pass.

When I saw Chick Corea play the piano and I sensed that he did not know there was anyone else in the auditorium.

The fifth-grade class made up entirely of second-generation immigrants from Mexico that I taught art to. The boy who stood up at the back of the class when I showed one of my paintings and exclaimed with more sincerity than any person has used to react to my art, "That is beautiful!"

The sadness I do not understand, of which there is so much. The hope that I might not only understand some of that despair, but that in some way I might also find a way to alleviate it.

The faith that my burdens of sorrow have been lightened by someone I do not know.

The morning it rained and my children noticed how happy the trees looked, and immediately went outside to get soaked.

Celebration.

All my son wanted for his birthday was a few people to love him. At exactly 5:00 p.m. the candles were lit, and dozens of people from our neighborhood hunkered over the cake. They sang, ate, and left to play on the grass or talk, all within five minutes. We participate in the sacraments of celebration even before we are well versed in humanity.

As a missionary I found myself skeptical of every old woman who told us she walked and talked with God all day. But then, who was I to say they did not? I feel pressed to say I do not believe in miracles because I picture my credibility in the world outside of spiritual belief dissipating in thin musterings of explanation. But the fact is, I am a spiritual being who does believe in miracles, not because I am required to see them, but because my choosing to find them has, at the most simple level, made me happy.

One night last summer I lay awake in bed; my husband was gone on fieldwork, my children were sleeping in the next room, and my parents whose house we were staying in for the summer were upset about something. The following morning I was to arise early and drive to the hospital for a medical procedure. It would not have been a big deal except that I faint at the simple sight of a needle. I was sick to my stomach thinking about it, and I was alone. I had not been in the practice of scripture reading for some time, and prayer was infrequent, but this night I took a moment to both pray and let my scriptures fall open with familiar faith in the divine. My page opened to 3 Nephi 13.

Take therefore no thought for the morrow, for the morrow shall take thought for the things of itself.

And so, my spirituality remains in the space between the complexity of belief and the poignant experiences that point to something far more than myself, a rich heritage of mothering and fathering that somehow orchestrates coincidence into miracle time and time again.

DURING THE FIRST nervous mile of my first half marathon I noticed through the crowd one particular runner. Perhaps it was the fact that she was just as curvy as I, or perhaps it was that I'd run all my practice miles with a dear friend and knew the necessity of companionship. Whether it was the Spirit speaking to me, or my own spirit demanding the togetherness I'd become so accustomed to, I felt I should go and run with her.

Slowly we neared each other as runners passed us and as we passed runners. Our movements started to sync, and by

mile three, I was pretty sure we were running together. At mile seven we still had not so much as glanced at one another, and I wondered what she thought about the girl next to her. I took a gummy chew out of my back pocket, bit off half, and offered her the other half while we continued to run. She reached out and accepted it, and then I knew we would finish the race together.

For the next six miles we paced with each other. She jogged in place while I retied my shoes. I walked with her when she slowed down up the hills. We walked together, still without a glance or word between us up the foreboding incline of mile eleven as music blasted in our respective headphones. I wondered what she was listening to. In the final mile my strength was gone, and I thought I might have to stop, but the stranger I had run the whole race with gave me a thumbs-up.

We crossed the finish line together, and then upon stopping we turned and hugged tightly, sweat dripping down our necks and backs. She said, "I could not have done this without you." I was surprised to hear she had a strong accent. Her name was Rose. We took a photograph together, hugged once more. It will be a miracle if we ever run into one another again in this life.

I hesitate to squeeze this experience into the box of Mormonness or spirituality. Mostly I just want it to be what it was: a sacred thirteen-mile run with a stranger of a different ethnicity, background, and world from me. Then again, everything I understand about Latter-day Saint theology points to the idea that I am not to work out my salvation alone, but that reliance on other people and their reliance on me is a crucial part of our work. Maybe I do not need to go on hoping that everyone in my church will think like me. Maybe even in our differences we can look each other in the eyes and say sincerely, "I could not do this without you."

A S A VERY YOUNG MOTHER, I lived in Sweden while my husband worked at the university there. During the days we were pioneers navigating in a quiet and beautiful land. It was wonderful. Carl had to leave each morning during those two weeks to lead a field camp and was unreachable. I did not know a single person in Sweden, and everyone I could call at home slept while we were awake. It was the most alone I have ever felt in my whole life. I had lived abroad before, and I had been on my own before, but I was not quite prepared to be so alone or to see my kids feel so alone.

One day, to people who would likely never read my thank you, I wrote this:

"Please be broadly and unsuspectingly kind. Be guardian to those around you, however briefly they are yours. I think you will find it more natural than you think. Protect the people that come into your space, even when you do not know what they need protecting from."

Jesus makes a striking statement in Matthew 10:8 that I cannot shake. "Freely ye have received, freely give." How freely indeed I have received, often with eagerness and without a look back. How ashamed to realize how often I am reluctant to freely give.

So from Pauline, the woman from Kenya with the black lab who invited us in and let Remy jump on her couch and dig for worms among her vegetables; from the kind woman with the leather saddle shoes who translated the whole church meeting for me without my asking; from the man at the grocery store who asked first in Swedish, then in English, if I needed help out to the car with my bags, I have freely received, drunk, gulped up your kindness. How could you have known your words and gestures would be a lighthouse in the sometimes wavering and lonely night of life?

There is such a thing as the friendless and the helpless. I know, because those words have described me in times past. I think we all are vulnerable to this, even in the midst of a crowd. Time moves like cycling seasons in the course of a week, a day, or even an hour. We can be our worst and our best a dozen times in a single day.

And so, like the way Thea wakes at 3:00 a.m. and holds

her arms up in the dark knowing I will reach down to her and slide my hands under her familiar and heavenly shoulders and pull her close, look for those who need your love and pull them quickly and close to you. Let them know it will be all right because you too have been told so by someone else at some sacred time a thousand times over.

THE MISSIONARIES that lived in the house before we moved in warned us not to feed the three-legged dog. He will never leave you, they said. One crust of bread, some lentils from the bottom of the pan against better judgment one evening, and he came back every morning. Hobbling around the crumbling cement corner of the building, expectant and droopy-eyed. As we left the apartment one morning, I saw his body, round ribs raising a prayer then falling back down again, curled in the colorless patio, pushed tight against the wall for a little warmth. What is it about a useless, hopeful creature that nestles deep in the heart? Perhaps they are the secret keepers of the unreasonable faith we want to have.

We walked past the butcher's shop, and I sorted the smells, still only bordering on familiar, part homesick, Jesus fresh on my mind. Maybe that dog knew somewhere in the muddy slums close by there were three friends who would come fetch him one night, then lower him through a hole in a roof into a crowded room where a man was speaking. He had to interrupt everything for a quick miracle. I hoped I'd be there to see him. I'd scratch behind his ears one last time before he ran out the door, full legged and barking tidings of great joy.

REMY DID NOT want to go to preschool because he claimed that no one wanted to play with him. When we got to his classroom, he plopped down to play with some blocks, and a fuzzy-headed girl I've never noticed sat next to him. She shoved over a little card she had made specifically for him at home, his name in sparkly stickers at the top. Clearly, his needs had been anticipated long before I knew they existed. I got teary-eyed as I turned to see their two heads bent and playing before I walked out the door.

I was, of course, teary-eyed at the immensity of knowing that in some way, by some force I do not understand, I am so often cared for in ways I could not have thought to ask for. But more, it was because I realized it had been too long since I'd let a small experience like that enter my heart and simply rest there.

At times, my cynicism has been a guest that overstays its welcome. For the past few years, my spiritual life has been examined through two lenses: one magnifies the magnificent and leaves me speechlessly in love with my children, my husband, the forests, the ocean, the people in my ward who speak and do with sincerity and patience, my students, my neighbors, the belief that I can do good and important things using the gospel of Jesus Christ as my compass. The other lens, which has been equally useful and vital in my adult spiritual upbringing, is a lens of serious questioning, pulling apart, recontextualizing, opening doors to sometimes find anger, resentment, confusion, or hurt standing guard over my spirituality.

I am most at peace when I look through both of these lenses simultaneously to examine my spiritual life. It is and will continue to be difficult to reconcile the fact that my spiritual life will likely never again be the simple magic of certainty that I was lucky enough to experience for a long season in my younger years. At the same time, I am not equipped to move forward carrying solely the questions, however bravely I shoulder them. Pretending the questions are not a part of my spiritual life clouds my vision. A prayer I did not even realize I had been saying was answered when I saw Remy directly validated in a way he needed so badly, and the holiness of that moment was almost refracted out of focus by my lens of cynicism.

The questions are important, but they are not everything.

Hurt, anger, and resentment are real and not created of demons, but of a human heart—the same heart that longs for hope and belief, and on many occasions has been met with their miraculous delivery. Looking through both the lens of hope and the lens of questioning requires active examination of my experiences. Looking through both lenses requires me not simply to see, but to ask why and how and to be humbled and grateful when I find the answer is always "because We love you."

Speak

THE SOUND OF PAPERS over a century old, which is to say brittle, yellowed, stacked, and worn so they no longer lay flat but rather like the fluffy quilts at the foot of my grandparents' bed. I had been in the special collections in the basement of Brigham Young University's library for hours reading journals of Mormon women who lived before the turn of the twentieth century. I had come to this place with visions of a spiritual feast. In my naive imaginings I was sure I was about to uncover the secrets of what it was to have perfect faith in the gospel of Jesus Christ. That first day I read journal entries by Emmeline B. Wells in her own pretty handwriting from the time she was a teenager through the decades until she was an old woman. The journals were consistent, filled with the day to day, and not at all what I had expected from a woman I'd learned to hold up on a holy pedestal of righteousness.

Emmeline did not live in a state of constant spiritual grandeur. In fact, many of her journal entries expressed anger at the loss of family members, disappointment in her church experiences, frustration in her callings, annoyance with people she worked with. There was also a salt and peppering of testimony, a handful of entries expounding moments of complete faith, with many quotidian moments in between. That first afternoon, I walked up the stone stairs of the library and out into the bright day carrying the burden of disillusionment. The journals were not at all what I thought they would be but rather far more filled with doubt.

If this remarkable woman did not have Mormonism figured out, then how could I ever expect to? The story Emmeline wove for herself by the end of her life was complex and imperfect. It was disconcerting to me, a girl who had placed hope and value in the understanding of the women I'd read about in Young Women and Relief Society. But the more I rolled Emmeline's words over in my head, the more I realized that yet another myth of perfection from a character in church history was precisely the thing I did not need. I needed characters that, even across the many years' difference, could tell me that they understood. Entry after entry became evidence that my own struggles were valid, her honesty an example I could follow.

As I went back to the special collections many days that summer, the imperfect, questioning, fiery women I read about did much more to preserve my hope in Mormonism than any pedestalized example of perfection and complete understanding might have done. These women became my friends—their stories, forever forward, a bit of my own.

I LOVED the one female seminary teacher out of the dozen that taught at the small brick seminary building in the parking lot of our school. We teased her about not being married, and she was a good sport about our naïveté. When she did get married, then pregnant soon after, we students were full of happiness right along with her. At the time I was only vaguely aware of the policy disallowing a mother of young children from teaching seminary, so it was startling to actually come back one semester and see Sister Miller's classroom taken over by a stranger. I lost a sense of camaraderie to have her gone. I think we all did, not just the girls, but the boys too.

This policy was changed in 2014. Now women can be full-time seminary teachers even with children at home. It feels like a moment for celebration—even if long overdue—each time we, as a culture, create space and power to voices that have long been more quiet than others. More and more I feel an imperative to speak and to help others around me speak. The body of Christ flourishes when each part is heard and listened to.

I GREW UP in a place where driving to another city meant passing one hundred billboards along the way. They tiresomely advertised plastic surgery and weight loss, selling a brand of beauty we are encouraged to want but do not have. After Remy was born, and my new body was far from billboard expectations but ideal in every other human way, I became even more tired of the false and unhelpful expectations that constantly showed up without invitation.

I believe in taking stewardship of the place in which we find ourselves, so I applied for a grant to receive funding to replace some of the city's billboards with the work of local poets. A professor and I were awarded the grant money and began work to follow through on the project with relish. As we read through dozens of poems submitted by local writers, one in particular stood out. The poem was called "Small Prayer," a quiet poem with lines like "There is a bird in the woods whose song stops you/ in a field of tulips," concluding with "Amend, *thank you*, amen."

With the help of a designer, we spread the poem's lines across three successive billboards. Carl and I stood below the billboards on the side of the dusty Utah highway while a worker climbed the rungs and unrolled the giant poem word by word. I was so proud to see each of them revealed—"thank you," "amen," "bird in the woods," together looking down at us from places that previously offered me nothing but diminished self-esteem and the belief that I needed to be someone different than who I already was in order to be happy. Our new son slept on my chest in a carrier, and I thought how it is for him, for the people who are so young in this world, that this battle on behalf of edifying ideas and messages is worth fighting.

The day the billboards went up, my professor and I, along with a group of artists and writers from the community, hosted art and poetry workshops all over the city where people showed up to create paintings and write their stories together. In the culminating event, we embarked from an empty parking lot, a large caravan of cars driving past the billboards together, honking and waving to celebrate opening night. I had not yet met the person whose poem was selected. He stood at the foot of the first billboard, leaning against the giant stalk of metal with his creation perched on top. He was emotional to see his words so big. He could not stop thanking my professor and me. He said he had recently been divorced, was jobless and without wind in his sails. He did not know what he could offer anyone, but there we all were, standing bravely on a freeway against the mountains of the city we grew up in, a hundred strangers honking and reading his poem. I found a great confidence and joy in taking ownership of the spaces I had so long been a part of but had not yet made my own.

The billboard poetry night ended at a park where families with small children, women in high heels, curious neighbors, friends, many people I'd never seen before gathered. High school students set up an art show in a portable gallery they had built, a local caterer served fresh peaches and homemade bread to the crowd, and the rest of the poets read their poem submissions.

Later the winning poet stood in front of the crowd and spoke about what it means to have a community support you, to acknowledge your thoughts and emotions. It is lifeblood. Each of us are stewards of our place and also of the people in our proximity. I continue working to listen through the noise until I hear my own voice, and then I trust that voice. I trust it will create purposeful occasions of grace.

SOME WOMEN WHOSE STORIES I HAVE KNOW OR AM GETTING TO KNOW

Patricia Christensen. Mary Elizabeth Monahan. Emma Smith. Minerva Teichert. Chieko Okazaki. Lucy Mack Smith. Anne Bradstreet. Elizabeth Bishop. Patty Bartlett

Sessions. Eleanor Roosevelt. Belle Spafford. Emmeline B. Wells. Esther Peterson. Lola Bickmore. Beulah Larsen. Laurel Thatcher Ulrich. Claudia Bushman. Terry Tempest Williams. Alice Louise Reynolds. Esther Peterson. Eliza R. Snow. Aung San Suu Kyi. Dorothy Canfield. Emily Dickinson. Virginia Woolf. Marie Curie. Marie Tharp. Maya Angelou. Mother Teresa. Noor Inayat Khan. Rosa Parks. Annistacia Potter. Lydia Hurst. Emma Day. Qiu Jin. Rosalind Franklin. Ruby Bridges. Sojourner Truth. Wilma Rudolph. Annie Dillard. Marilynne Robinson. Joyce Carol Oates. Louisa Barnes Pratt. Harriet Tubman. Irena Sendler. Jane Goodall. Amy Hone. Sharon Meyers. Karen Jackson. Becky Angus. Shelly Norton. Rita Christensen. MarieAnne Hoiland. Sage Rabino. Bayley Goldsberry. Mary Ann Christensen. My Heavenly Mother. Myself.

I HEARD IT ONCE said that Mother Teresa experienced several profound spiritual experiences before enduring fifty years of silence when the heavens were sealed to her. How comforting to find such kinship with a holy woman of another tradition. I sometimes wonder where the beaming sense of God I once had has gone.

When I was in kindergarten, I frequently played a game with my best friend where we would sit on the grass out by my mailbox and wonder about God. We pictured him as a giant, maybe a giant with wings and a shining face. I remember telling my friend, "God's bellybutton is the size of a trashcan." Until recent years, that God, the one I imagined pushing back plump clouds to reach out and whisper to me, was very present in my life.

On my mission in particular. The skies in Uruguay were more expansive and encompassing than any I had seen before or since. I often felt like a tiny doll in a glass globe. There seemed to be so much space in that sky for God to reach down and talk to me. I felt positive that he led us to certain doors and to talk to specific people on the street. I longed for this thin-veiled relationship in the months and years after my mission, but it slowly faded except for brief lightning-flash moments. The talkative God I seemed to know so well grew quiet in my life, and in the absence I have found an uprising of the *godly*.

This is not to say I do not believe God is there. I do. As a Mormon, I believe I am a child of heavenly parents. I believe they are kind and concerned and somehow woven into the details and emotions of my life and the world in ways I cannot fully comprehend. I believe there are times they weep for me, both because of our nearness and because of our distance. I believe this because I do the same for my own children.

The God of my youth's understanding, however, with

the trashcan belly button, with the direct line from heaven straight to me through the skies of Uruguay, seems quiet. I think in some ways I made my heavenly parents out to be more garish than they ever intended and assumed that they must be ready to offer a spectacular fanfare of answers and miracles always. I think the God I understood in my youth knew just what I needed—I needed that God—and I'm learning to trust that God continues to know so now.

I am no Mother Teresa, but in these past years I still felt rushes of solitude wash over my spirituality—tide in, tide out. At first it alarmed me, and I often felt like I was scrambling to hold fast to the profundity that buoyed me up when I was younger. There were—there still are—many, many times when I am jarred by my smallness and lack of understanding. I sometimes feel like I have lost something and cannot put a finger on where I have left it. I sometimes call out for God as I knew God in my youth, the one who felt less reserved, more quick to offer me answers. I still believe in a God who holds me in a tender hand's palm, only in different ways than before, surrounded by palpable evidence so close around me.

I created a space in my heart for questions. They are now part of my religious dialogue when for so long I would usher them out the door before allowing them to catch their breath. I felt relief when I spoke to them and bid them welcome. I learned those questions were not so bad after all—they were sincere truth seekers rather than the wily tricksters I had believed them to be. And now there are so many things I have not even thought to ask yet.

For so long, the quick tears I shed when asked to share my testimony of God led me to believe that I understood. It was really all quite simple. I cry far less often now in such moments, and at first I was shaken up to think my heart had turned cold. But my heart is not cold; it is beating warm, wildly. The questions are not always stumbling blocks but often thoughts and ideas for us to acknowledge, to kneel beside and say a prayer right alongside. Doubt too, can be part of a holy experience.

There is a hallowed and well-trodden path between heart and mind that, though complicated, can be the surest track to the ephemeral beauty this world has to offer. Like the evening when Remy and Thea were bathed, pajamaed, and hair-combed, wrestling and laughing on my bed. There is no amount of God calling down from the heavens or tapping me on the shoulder that could equal my joy, or school me more effectively in the art of spontaneous love, than in seeing those two babies in their tiny bodies learning what it is to be alive in this world.

How else to explain this quiet God? Part of Carl's work as a geologist involves the process of dating grains of sand—

tiny zircons—to better understand ancient landscapes. After working through hundreds, sometimes thousands, he slowly puts back together a picture and story of how those grains of sand came to be where they are after millions of years, a conglomerate of all their varied and vast histories. Carl can say, for example, "This zircon was once part of a granite that was at the top of a mountain range that has since eroded, redeposited, and later uplifted into a mountain and eroded again, only to be washed down a series of streams, crushed and broken along the way until it finally rested for a moment," at which point Carl picked it up, worked it over, and dated it in an attempt to unravel its story. And the next zircon may tell a different story entirely. How then, could God simply speak these kinds of miracles to me the way I believed they had been before? Pure awe escapes vocabulary. Perhaps that explains the quiet.

Perhaps this is merely an attempt to comfort myself, to appease the part of me that wants to believe that the silence of God is not punishment or worse. I am still learning to believe that the quietness of God is the substance of trust, that it is part of a season of deep love in which the godly in my daily life usurps the need for God to speak loudly. And that, I can learn to celebrate.

THE WEEK I had been reading about a city in Thailand that is built almost entirely on the premise of sex trafficking was the same week our Relief Society lesson was about the importance of temple marriage. I sat in my pastel-cushioned folding chair and let the wide-eyed baby next to me investigate my fingers one at a time. As the lesson unfolded, the context suddenly felt existential and confusing, and I wanted to excuse myself. I pictured myself nudging past the covered knees of the women I had grown up with, then going outside to sit under a tree to pray, or just be silent—

I stayed.

Words like *worthy* and *blessed* seemed incomprehensible as I thought about the women who lived in that distant Thailand city. I knew I could not understand their life at all, what it must feel like to live in a city built on sex trafficking, but I know something of what it is to be a woman—to love, want, hope, and work as a woman, and so my mind wandered the streets hoping to find one of them to hug, to help, to offer a word of hope.

I could not find a comfortable space for my thoughts to settle as the discussion focused on temple worthiness, what we must and must not do, what we must change about ourselves, what we must repent of. I knew the conversation stemmed from a place of love and respect. I endeavor to be worthy of the temple—but those women in Thailand. Those women . . .

I could not stop thinking about how they would more than likely never set foot in a celestial room. Circumstances would prevent their being worthy, and I felt a tension build so sharply in my heart and mind that the voice inside me— the me in a dress with the lesson book open on my lap, who dressed her children to come to church, who sat through sacrament meeting desperate to keep those kids reverent, who raised her hand to volunteer for things at the beginning of class—screamed inside, a scream made up of a dozen emotions, rattling even the quietest parts of my spirit. The conversation in the room went on around me, and I did not know what to think, until suddenly, for a brief moment, I did.

I felt tired of feeling selfish and thinking about myself. I did not want to talk about going to the temple for myself or even for my ancestors then. I wanted to talk about how my temple worthiness could better make me an instrument of peace in corners of the world that do not have peace. What if in some way I could actually make life better for those women and girls in Thailand by getting myself to the temple to receive inspiration? I wanted the work of my own salvation to have less to do with me and more to do with what I might offer others.

That fleeting moment of personal understanding felt so

real. It altered my approach to personal spiritual practices. It is worthwhile to think of how I can sit here at church in the same table-covered-with-a-lacy-pastel-cloth, chalk-boarded, folding-chair-lined, piano-at-the-front room and have a vastly different experience than the person next to me or behind me or in front of me, though I have little way of knowing exactly what those varied experiences are. Maybe the dissonance I sometimes encounter here is what keeps me returning each week. Maybe that scream I heard inside me was not born only of frustration, but of the spirit. I return to the spirituality that I know best because I believe it can teach me how to serve and make the world better. The wild yell I felt inside is just as important as the still small voice that translated it. Perhaps they could be one and the same.

WE HAD A LESSON in my Young Women class about preparing to receive a patriarchal blessing. The idea that God had a plan for my life, that I could get a shot at knowing some of it, intrigued me. My mom set up an appointment at the patriarch's home, and I dove into what I understood to be proper preparation for such an event. I took it as seriously as a fifteen-year-old could—praying, reading scriptures, trying to be righteous at home and school—but honestly a part of me was driven by simple curiosity to see if my blessing would mention a husband.

There were rumors of girls whose blessings made no mention of marriage, and I was slightly terrified that I could be one of them. I fasted the whole day before my blessing, which made me a little short-tempered. I snapped at my sister, then felt as if I'd driven the spirit of revelation away—surely I would not be given a promise of marriage with an attitude like that.

The day arrived, and the kind patriarch invited us into his home where he and his wife welcomed my whole family into a living room that displayed every trope of Mormon culture—framed paintings of Jesus, Relief Society crafts, family photographs, a family tree diagram filled in with the slanted writing of a woman—all of which was a comfort to me.

The patriarch placed shaking and wrinkled hands on my head and prayed about my future mission, spouse, children, and offerings to the world while his wife transcribed his words. The experience was special, and the blessing did give voice and confidence to that eccentric and newly teen-aged girl with a propensity for writing and art. Along with marriage, I was promised many other things I had not yet valued as deeply as the promise of a husband—intellect, work, writing, personal revelation, children, service, advocacy.

I received the blessing, hand-typed, a few weeks later in the mail. The folded paper inside felt sacred. I felt grateful to the giver of the blessing but hardly gave a second thought to the one also in the room who valiantly listened and recorded every word of it for me. It took me many years to wonder about the patriarch's wife and her role in the event of my blessing. I wondered what advice she might have offered me, what the spirit might have prompted her to pass on. I wish her feminine role in that moment had asked more of her than to type the words she heard her husband speak. I want to go back and listen more carefully. In the pauses I want to hear my own voice asking her, "What is your story? Won't you tell it to me?"

LETTER FOR MY DAUGHTER, THEA

FOR MY BIRTHDAY we went to the beach. Not a sandy beach, but a secret rocky beach down a path rife with poison oak that we jumped over. The day was a little bit foggy, a little bit colorless, a little bit cold. I walked along behind Carl, Remy, and you, stopping to pick up a fossil of a shell, a piece of abalone, a memory of my son looking out into the vast ocean. We had been collecting quietly, sliding over wet rocks, filling our pockets with treasure for almost an hour when you, all of three years, came and sat next to me. I noticed your little palm was tightly shut, and when I asked what you had, you opened your hand to reveal a dozen carefully selected round pebbles. You have a propensity for treasuring small spherical objects, and I welled up with intense pride and love as I pictured you, my devout little girl, searching, examining, holding on to the very best things without even the intention to show me unless I asked.

Thea, as a girl it was hard for me to speak out of fear for saying the wrong thing, or fear of being too bold or even too soft. As a grown woman it is sometimes even more difficult. But please, let your wandering spiritual impressions take shape and then give them a voice, even if they happen between the odd hours of making casseroles and bathing children, or on the days of feeling alone and without direction, in a workspace, or through sleepless nights. Speak, even when you are sure there is someone smarter and more informed than you in the room. Give credence to your spiritual ideas. Allow a bit of chaos to reign within your thoughts, and then let that unexpected happiness spill into the spaces around you. Your story carries power. Your experience is valid. Your voice is vital. I think back on that moment on the beach, and I want so much for your first impulse not to be simply to siphon away the palm full of precious and strong pebbles that miraculously tumbled to you from a vast and completely wild earth. I want your first impulse to be to open your hand and talk about how you found them, to let them shine out like rising firelight on a dark hillside.

Laughter

EIGHT TIMES I LAUGHED AS A MORMON

THE TIME MY FRIEND told me to pull her finger right before the tree-of-life hike through the trees at camp, and she tooted loudly, and the leaders pretended not to hear, and into the woods we went, stifling laughter into our jacket sleeves, all too aware that we were wholly irreverent. So many nights sitting in my family living room at the end of the day when someone started to pray and did not finish, but ended in laughter for no reason until my sisters, brother, parents, and I were all laughing for no reason as well. Watching old Book of Mormon cartoon videos. When my husband dressed up as Moses in an old robe and cotton beard and stood in front of the Primary pretending to see a burning bush. At family barbeques with all my aunts and uncles. At the annual roadshow when all the Young Men leaders performed a hip-hop dance. As a missionary when I spent a whole six weeks posing for photos only to find the camera was empty of film; my companion and I laughed so hard we nearly fell to the ground. The time I was supposed to sing Father's Day songs in sacrament meeting, and as I stood there in my eleven-year-old body, an overgrown dandelion towering a full head above all the children, I was suddenly aware of the absurdity. I stood there, in front of the whole audience, stifling laughter while trying to mouth the songs, without a place to hide or an exit to make. I did not sing to my dad. I laughed and laughed without an end in sight to him. My mom put on her rare serious face after and told me I owed him a serious apology, but really, I cannot think of something that would please him more than to know his daughter was no stranger to laughter in places where God is also found. He once told me that he ran into a friend in the celestial room of the temple, and for no explainable reason they found themselves in the corner laughing hysterically—silently—for the duration of their stay.

M Y GRANDPARENTS thought they would be called to a lovely mission because they had been to London once and felt their destiny would lead them back to comfortable benches in green parks. When they received their call to an Indian reservation in South Dakota, they were slightly taken aback, if only in their vision of what they presumed themselves to be. But they went with vigor, right into the major snowstorms that covered their little RV like a white potato bug on an empty plain. They tunneled their way out of the door each morning and then set to the task of helping in whatever way they could—shoveling other people out of their homes, giving rides, organizing activities for the youth, imparting what little financial wisdom they had to struggling parents in the ward.

One of the few relics I cherish from their mission is a photograph they sent home of my grandpa in a full costume for a ward skit. He is surrounded by a group of church members, all partly out of place as they huddle together in the church gym's poor lighting. My grandpa is beaming—the smile I recognize from the black-and-white photographs of his early college years when the whole world was made for him.

One summer afternoon my aunt received a phone call from my grandma. At first my aunt worried because it was against the rules to call home, and she worried again when, in the place of my grandma, all she could hear was muffles and attempts to talk. Grandma finally got out the words through fits of crying laughter that Grandpa had been trapped on the riding lawnmower for two hours, and there was no sign of him stopping. With great goodwill and a love for obedience, he had hopped on and revved up that beast of a machine before realizing he had no idea how to turn it off. My grandma said all she had seen for two hours was a cloud of dust as he plowed over the rolling hills, him returning back and again, his few strands of hair blowing valiantly in the air. We later learned that he finally came to a stop in a tangle of wires a couple of acres over and had knocked out the power in a nursing home.

My grandparents passed away months before I left on my own mission, and so I did not get to write home to them about all the times I laughed. Still, when I think of their lives now, I think of how laughter was woven into so many of the stories that meant the most to them. I think of the way that joy was their motive, not just for them, but for the people they encountered. I want to be fueled by the hope for joy for myself and others—laughter coloring the stories I will have to tell when I am old.

ALONG WITH so many young women growing up with me, I was jealous and frustrated that the young men and scouts in my ward hiked, rock climbed, and river rafted while I longed to do anything of the sort. It still upsets me, but the other ways in which I was cared for by my leaders is still invaluable. At the time I could not calculate their sacrifice in spending hours with me and the other girls in my ward each week when they had busy adult lives. I did not yet understand the value of having a community of women to watch over me.

My Young Women leaders, intelligent and kind-hearted, unintentionally gifted me insight into motherhood and womanhood as they talked among themselves at our weekly activities of baking, sewing, and covering a leader's doors in paper hearts. On rare occasions I would catch a glimpse of the turbulent and shining worlds of these women in more public settings, like when they delivered sacrament meeting talks, but I learned so much more about what it is to be a woman and a Latter-day Saint in the accidental sermons they delivered to eavesdroppers at Young Women activities.

I loved their candid expressions—one leader both lamented and laughed about the chaos of having twin toddlers, another leader spoke about her work with a nonprofit organization, another updated the others about her progress in earning a PhD in statistics. They talked about their missions, college, dating, and on rare occasion their fears.

One woman was married but never had children and still, to this day, she decorates the front door of my parents' home for me every single birthday, exactly the way she has since I was twelve. Packs of Smarties and streamers taped to photocopied signs in her handwriting still fill me with the comfort that I was always noticed by someone. She is a legend of kindness in our neighborhood, spending whole days taking young women to buy school clothes, helping to plant a garden in a backyard, or just sitting on her couch watching old films. When a girl in our ward lacked the legal documentation necessary to go to college or get a job, this woman invited her over every afternoon to do jobs at the house, study with her, and every once in a while to get a makeover at the mall.

Some of my leaders had married young, some were not married, one was divorced, one had stepchildren, some showed up to our activities with a baby in tow, and we could not get enough of imagining the glorious lives these women around us were living—jobs and babies and marriages. It was a privilege to be on the inside loop where these women spoke so freely together about their lives. Such a community of women is exuberant with collective ideas. The group who watched over me as a youth created a kaleidoscope of experiences, but laughter, above all, is what I remember best from them. It is the sound Thea hears when my friends and I gather together now. It is the sound of camaraderie and sisterhood, of joy.

Better/Hope/Faith

M Y LIFE is punctuated by parentheses. Spaces and moments that are not the main point, not the absolute essential, and which rarely end with an exclamation mark. Pieces that are inserted right in the middle of things, causing us pause, asking us to reconsider what was said before and after. I think of these curved parenthetical lines as protective walls intentionally put up amid routine and chaos. I think of my current parent self as author, the creator of curated paragraphs for the little babes who rely on intuition and the whirring wings inside their little bodies.

On a car ride home from a friend's house, I decided what matters to me more than my own cynicism is softness. A soft heart is what I want. I put on some choral music as soundtrack for our drive home through the suburbs. The moon was round and layered in a quilt of clouds. Remy had gotten his shirt muddy, so he was bare-chested with black-and-white striped pants, and in the rearview mirror I could see his round face looking back at him against the dark window. Thea moved her arms in slow circles. We drove for a while without talking, and then I sensed Remy wanted to say something. I turned down the music, and he said, "Mom, Jesus is close by here. He is in my mind telling me to do good things, and I'm listening." All I could muster from the front seat was, "That's nice, Remy."

I stumble over my words. I do not know how to voice the complexities of both my faith and doubt to my four-year-old with my limited language, and so, often, I say nothing at all. I have spent a lot of time worrying that I do him a disservice by not articulating every nuance of my belief and unbelief. But tonight I understood that my words will always be secondary to what he can learn to hear himself.

I am a maker of parentheses, pockets of safety and peace wherein my children can nestle into themselves and listen. It is not my job to tell them what to hear or understand there, but rather to simply trust it. I think of our car ride home as a brief parenthetical moment in our day. That is my job, to every now and then listen carefully enough to know when a sentence needs pause and to be brave enough to employ the proper grammar, to place that rounded wall, a deliberate sacred space. The world is full of run-on sentences, of exclamation marks and words that are not well thought out. The world will not so easily offer my children that space to pause and breathe, to look at their reflection in the window with the moon high above and believe that Jesus is in their head, telling them to do the best things.

ONCE ON A NEW YORK subway soon after my mission, I got talking with a kid around my age about religion. I said I was Mormon, and he asked me what made us different. We had three stops to go, so I set about giving a speedy first lesson as I'd done for eighteen months. I should have been used to rejection, but a stubborn and hopeful part of me that refuses to be extinguished still expected some sort of miracle, a light to descend on the boy and those grimy old subway seats. It did not. My words were far from eloquent, and I saw the boy's face change from curiosity to confusion. And then he was getting up and heading out into the dank darkness of the subway stop.

That was over ten years ago, but I still feel a pang of guilt about failing him, for not helping him to feel a little bit of God's love but instead bombarding him with a lot of words and concepts. Not too long ago I met an old man at the cookie table after a church fireside. He told me how he had left the church for thirty years, gotten married, had children, and then got very sick. There in the hospital he promised God that if he got better he would return to church and not leave.

He did and lived in a Boston ward for twenty-five years. When they moved back to San Francisco, his wife, who was a devout Catholic, said one day, "Promise me something? Please promise me that you will keep going to your church."

He asked her why on earth she would ask that of him when she had no interest in the church herself. She simply said, "You are a better person when you do."

I wish I could meet that boy from the subway again, and when he asked his question, "So what makes Mormons different?" I would not jump straight into expounding the doctrine. I would simply tell him that there is something about the ideas in the Book of Mormon that make me want to be a better neighbor, mother, and wife. The story of Joseph Smith has allowed me to pursue a relationship with heavenly parents that I might not know to look for otherwise, and mostly I would tell him that I do not know so much, but I do know I am a better person when I am here.

I OFTEN FIND myself at a crossroads between the abstraction of spirituality and the everyday practicality necessitated by a religion. I find myself wanting to say that I know things without a doubt and then stumbling back at the grandiosity of my own supposition. I think of seeing the red fox that lives near my parents' house who comes down from the hills on so rare an occasion. Once, more than half a decade

ago, I saw him cross the road and dart down into a deep gully full of brush, but not before we spent a moment watching each other. His dark eyes seemed equal parts fear, curiosity, and delight. It was probably around the same time the scaffolding of my youthful faith was coming down.

For him, his wild landscape was being rapidly replaced by townhomes and condominiums with a clubhouse and pool. The once quiet mountainside he must have known so well was now a buzzing space of human movement—dinners, fights, embraces, jobs, cars leaving driveways early in the morning, kids with clouded breath waiting at bus stops. One thing is replaced with another, over and over and over again.

At times, my despair has been replaced by the hopeful act of consuming blessed bread and water on Sunday, my skepticism likewise replaced by love when listening to a sincere talk or lesson. My childlike prayers have been deconstructed and reconstructed into the work of writing in faith that I will find God in surprising metaphors. Maybe the hardest thing to realize is, as with the fox, this spiritual landscape is not entirely mine, but that fact does not mean there are not wild pockets of untouched quiet inviting me to stop and stay while I sort out nothing more than the ways in which I am cared for.

WAYS IN WHICH I LOVED AND WAS LOVED DEARLY BY GAY MEN I DATED

I SAT IN HIS LIVING ROOM and we talked about poetry for hours every weekend while his parents slept upstairs. I sensed they were wary of me, of us alone downstairs. If only they knew how much we were really just talking about poetry, music, and art. I loved his little sister who thought I was a real artist before I thought I was. Up to that point, no boy wanted to date me based on the fact that I was good at talking about poetry and language. He told me he was gay one night while I sat on a wooden stool in my painting studio.

Much later when I would ask him about this moment, of course he remembered it in so much more detail than I. His bravery in telling exceeded my bravery in listening. After he told me, we drove to the place overlooking the valley we both grew up in, and we cried because we did not know what else to do, and then we laughed about having a crush on the same movie star.

One boyfriend taught me yoga—how to spread my fingers wide on the ground, how to love the way my body was stronger than I had ever believed. He taught me to leave the comfort of the indoors and go out to see the stars at night. Once, we spent a whole day making a fancy meal for my dad on his birthday and then invited my family to his cabin in the mountains. He played the violin, and we all clapped uproariously when he bowed at the end. For his birthday I gave him a small tree to plant at his cabin, and every so often I wonder how tall it has grown.

The pain experienced by someone who has a secret they feel they cannot tell runs deep like an underwater cave. I am forever indebted to these young men for allowing me to swim there, however briefly, with them.

I made one tenderhearted boy a birthday gift with all my favorite words letterpressed into thick paper. The process took hours and hours, setting each letter by hand, inking and pressing. Each run through the press was another tangible impression of how much I wanted him to be happy and to feel loved. He gave me bike rides through campus where I felt loved by a boy and giddy at the thought of a possible future with him.

One boy lived up the street from me, and everyone assumed we would date at some point. We had been inseparable through high school, and I was lost without him when he left on his mission. We would sneak out of our windows at night and roam the streets under the moonlight. After our missions it seemed the most obvious thing that we would date. One time a neighbor girl claimed she saw us through the window making out while we watched a movie, but that was never true. We found a mission tape he made for his family because he was sure he would die before he came home from Italy. He did not die, but I realized later, after he came out to me, that his greatest hope—a bargain with God to purchase with faithfulness a change of attraction—had been extinguished by the time he returned with honor. We talked of getting married but quickly realized it would not work. He sent me a quilt when Remy was born. Simple blues and purples, each square hand-stitched. I spread it over him each night of the first year of his life.

Years after I dated them and was married with children of my own, I wrote letters to say how much I loved each of them. They were there at significant turning points of my young life. They were the bright stars of a constellation only I can see. How I hope they are happy. I heard back from a few— kind words, familiar and articulate. I waited and waited for a response from the others, and when I heard nothing my heart broke again for the loss.

LETTER TO MY SON REMY

ONE AFTERNOON, you and I waited together at the bus stop on the small island in Sweden where we lived. Then we sat quietly in our seats, not disembarking until we found a trail into the woods. We walked for hours, and I watched you, my little boy, your tiny spirit shining under the canopy of trees, along the muddy trail.

That day, the dung beetle seemed an odd character to save, but I suppose you were charmed by the shimmer of blue on his back, his feet to air and kicking madly without traction, heaving against this deadly world until you came with your stick and delicately overturned each wriggling body one at a time, saving them from a fate they could not even consider as they trotted back to the horse's pile.

At one point we entered a meadow beneath a roof of leaves, the shape of which we had never seen, with an anthill taller than you and scurrying with surprising life—the afternoon light angling off in points, the whole forest a cathedral for our communion. This earth is not a mundane school. It is a journey with mentors who teach us about love in moments of refracted light in a meadow.

It began to rain, and we hiked down to the lake. Pings of water spread as far as we could see, stirring the water while delivering the promise a thousand times over:

These waters will be calm again.

My son, you are both a mentor and mentored in miracles and hope. The dung beetle, the light on the leaves before the storm, the way you held your hand up to the sky and let the rain pour over you.

IN 1989 A RAINBOW fell across the sky in our little neighborhood on the hill. I stood on the ledge of the bathtub
and curled my fingers on the windowsill to pull my scrawny
body up to see. I could hear voices, cadenced and sturdy,
through the open window. The rainbow was brighter than
any rainbow I have seen since, the sky more orange and
close. The fresh puddles on asphalt reflected two shimmer-
ing missionaries, pressed shirts and black pants, my mom,
my dad, my little white-haired brother between them, and
somewhere in the background me watching it all, document-
ing the magic, cataloging it for some future time.

Surely they all came inside to eat dinner then, and I
reached up on tiptoes and pulled on my best dress because
I always did when the missionaries came, and we must have
all celebrated my mom—after years of attending church on
and off, of listening to missionaries, of wondering, she decided to be baptized, and my dad had decided to come back
to be the one to baptize her. I do not know what changed
for my mom, except that she has spoken many times about
the way the people at church loved her, even before she was a
documented part of them.

In recent years the memory of a conversation I am not

sure I was supposed to hear at my Catholic aunt's house when she found out the news had resurfaced. My aunt was crying and asking my mom to reconsider, and my mom said, "I am happy—I am happy. You don't need to worry." I must have stitched those words into the part of me that wants so much to stay with the gospel of my upbringing. We were in this together from the beginning—my parents, my brother, sisters yet to come, the missionaries, and I—that ancient brand new rainbow emerging bright and triumphant after what must have been a rainstorm.

ONE HUNDRED BIRDS TAUGHT ME TO FLY

WINGSPAN OF MY GRANDMOTHER. Migration of my grandfather. My mother, nesting in a small yellow home. My father, pulling us in, feathers close around, keeping us safe. My cousin who lost a child, skimming the waters of heartache with golden wingtips. My neighbor, who gave her brightest feathers to every child in the neighborhood who came knocking on her door looking for a friend, yet still flew with ease. Clumsy take-off, beautiful recovery of my brother. My sister singing softly on a branch outside my window. My other sister, near her, steady and harmonizing. Constant morning song of my husband. First fluttering feathers of my

children as they stand at the edge of a nest. I whisper, *Go, the wind will carry you.* Remember the wildflowers we gathered, the fox we saw in the desert, the scramble up the thorny hill to the path that led us to the green meadow, the night we made shadows on a canyon wall, our arms like wings as we lifted them and pretended our shadows could fly.

FINDING

My son said, "I see fire in the sky."
I gave him sunset.
My daughter said she saw lightning on my dress,
a lion in the bushes at the farm,
the garbage truck coming to get her—again, again, I say no.
My children offer me ideas like wildflowers in a meadow,
and before I can stop myself, I am plucking the flowers
and replacing them with "stem," "petal," "leaf."
No to monsters, no to seeing Jesus in the church choir,
the boy next door is not actually your brother.
Yet somehow, each night, we kneel in their small bedroom,
my daughter closes her eyes and one by one lists off the things she loves
aloud:
the whales in the ocean, the wolves in the forest she has never seen,
the eucalyptus tree with the bugs in the bark, her bunk bed, her
brother.
Then my son promises, muffled into his lamb-like arms,
to be kind, to help someone if they are hurt, to listen to his holy ghost,
to try and be like Jesus.
When we finally say amen, we open our eyes,
and I sing the songs I know by heart
while the warm triangle of light
from the hall rests glittering in the doorway.

Epilogue

WHILE WRITING THIS BOOK

THE TREE OUTSIDE my bedroom window lost all its leaves, then grew new leaves, then seemed ready to float into the sky so buoyed up with white blossoms. I did dozens of loads of laundry. I prayed to have a softer heart and also a braver one. I knew I could not please everyone. I thought maybe I could but learned I cannot write my story with the intent to please. I stopped using the word *crisis* to describe my spiritual life. I discovered I was not in crisis—rather, I am an explorer. I was honest. I did not write about everything I wanted to. I erased. I rewrote. I got some lines right on the first try. I worked while my daughter napped and my son was at preschool. I worked at night after my children went to bed. I worked mostly at a corner table in the basement laundry room of our student housing. I got advice from friends. I listened carefully, both to those friends and to the whispering in my own heart. I learned to trust my story. I rearranged the book. I rearranged again and again. I worked as an art teacher in low-income schools. I babysat a lot of neighbor children. My children were babysat by the mothers of those children. I experienced spiritual highs. I experienced spiritual lows. I sat in a Relief Society lesson where we listed characteristics we imagine Heavenly Mother to have on the chalkboard. I sat through talks that felt difficult to hear. I talked with my husband about my doubts and fears about writing. My husband spent many late nights writing his dissertation. We laughed a lot. I took my children to the beach. I took my children to the park. I painted with them. I read library books with them. I went to a Catholic service to attend a sermon given by a woman I love to hear speak. I felt hope in the way cultural Mormonism will improve for my daughter and thereby also for my son. I felt discouraged in the way cultural Mormonism may not improve for my daughter and thereby also for my son. I talked with my parents on the phone. My mother-in-law came to my house for a few days so I could work. I cried when reading my writing. I laughed when reading my writing. I felt nervous. I wrote some pieces in anger but found they did not answer my questions or settle well inside the book. I wrote a few in anger—some that fit right in, others that I didn't want to continue to carry. I prayed in the mornings for help to write the words that are needed. I kept a notebook next to my bed. I hung a sign above the bike racks near my house that says "Take Courage" and saw it every day. I worried. I felt grateful. I read lots of poetry. I read my mission journals. I read scriptures. I read books by other people working out their own spirituality. I learned to trust the voices that have come before me and the ones that will come after and the ones that are speaking now. I called myself a feminist out loud. I felt a great love for the men who have directly supported this book and also me in unexpected and intuitive ways as I worked. I felt an ancient and sacred support of women from both the present and the past. I came to terms with possible failure despite my best effort. I came to terms with possible criticism. I thought of my children reading my words when they are my age. I thought of my grandma reading my words. I lost confidence then found it again. I walked in the rain. I changed. I learned a lot. I was wrong. I was right. I told my story. I realized that my story is not the point, but rather, that I can embrace the fact that every person has the starring role in their own story, that we are a million ways different. We are a field of wildflowers together when we tell our story. When I listen to the stories of others, when I cry not just for the hard parts of my own story, but for the hard parts in others', when I laugh together and love the stories I do not understand, when I recognize that my story is so small, but also so big, then I find Christ there. Then I picture myself entering a brightly colored room where everyone is cheering for me, not because I have figured out the answers but because I was brave enough to try. Then I see my mother, my father, my brother, my sisters, my husband, my children, my friends, my grandparents, my old boyfriends, my neighbors, and we are all cheering as each one comes through the door. Good job, we say. You are so loved, we say.

ACKNOWLEDGMENTS

This book is for the many people who believed I could fly long before I believed I could: My parents, May and Kent. My mother-in-law, Amy. My siblings, Dane, Sage, and Bayley. My aunts. My grandmother, Patty. My friends and mentors, Elisa, Kate, Zina, Sara, Dana, Brooke, Natania, Reija, Kim, Jason, Dan, Kristin, Annie, Lanee, Rachel, Kathy, Mei, and my brave editor, Blair. Without their kindness, I would be lost. There are many more names I wanted to put here, but please know if you think you belong here, you do.

I give my heart and thank-you to my husband Carl and my children, Remy and Thea, with whom I hope to fly into undetermined skies longer than we can imagine.